A PRENTICE HALL GUIDE TO

EVALUATING ONLINE RESOURCES

POLITICAL SCIENCE 2003

A PRENTICE HALL GUIDE TO

EVALUATING
<u>ONLINE</u>
RESOURCES

POLITICAL SCIENCE 2003

M. Neil Browne • Stuart M. Keeley
Bowling Green State University

Revised by Regina Swopes

PRENTICE HALL, UPPER SADDLE RIVER, NJ 07458

©2003 by PEARSON EDUCATION, INC.
Upper Saddle River, New Jersey 07458

ISBN 0-13-049631-6

Printed in the United States of America

Contents

Preface

Students rely increasingly on the Internet as their preferred resource for finding information and arguments. Indeed, our working title for this book was originally "I Found It on the Internet" because so many of our students had responded in that manner to us when we asked them the basis for some claim they had made. Their acceptance of Internet contentions was widespread and frightening.

We wrote this book because we saw no reason to think that this tendency to go to the Internet as a source for belief would be short-lived. On the contrary, the ease with which the Internet can be tapped for "knowledge" almost assures its frequent use.

As the authors of *Asking the Right Questions: A Guide to Critical Thinking*, we have already addressed in a fairly thorough fashion how the art of critical thinking can be applied to books, articles, lectures, and speeches. But we wanted these Internet books to address a different audience, one who needs a modified set of critical questions with which to process what they think they have learned from websites.

Critical thinking is a set of skills and attitudes for *evaluating* arguments. The arguments made on websites need especially careful assessment. The ease of access to the Internet makes it a medium where almost anything can be said, and often is. Hence, whatever we find on the Internet must be accepted only after we use all our critical tools to investigate the worth of the Internet claims. This book provides a series of techniques for doing exactly that investigation.

While we have also included information about the Internet and its features, we're pretty confident that most readers will already possess substantial knowledge about navigation on the Internet. Just in case that assumption is not true for particular readers, we have included enough Internet basics to bring every reader to a level of understanding of the medium such that the critical thinking skills herein can be useful. The primary purpose of the book, however, is to assist in developing a critical-thinking approach to the Internet.

The preparation of this edition was assisted by two talented and creative assistants, Elizabeth Barre and Justin Esarey. Both are much more than student assistants. Their devotion to high-quality work is inspirational to us as teachers.

Chapter 1

Finding Your Way

This thing that we now call the Internet has been evolving ever since it was first developed almost thirty years ago. Its prominence in our society has been increasing exponentially in recent years.

The Internet was born as the solution to a problem. It was designed to provide a global communication channel for the exchange of scientific information and research. Gradually, however, the Internet has also become a digital post office, a digital bulletin board, a digital telephone, and a digital tutor. Its real merit to you is how it will solve your problems and make your day just a bit more manageable. Hopefully, that is what you'll discover here.

Getting Started

The following URLs are a few of the many beginner's guides available on the Internet. You'll find everything you need to know about modems, browsers, e-mail, bulletin boards, chat rooms, and getting connected to the Internet on at least one of these sites:

An Introduction to the Internet from Interactive Connections
http://icactive.com/guide/index.htm
This is a very comprehensive guide to the Internet. It is provided by
Interactive Connections, an Internet Presence Provider. If you need a refresher course on Internet basics or are starting from scratch, then this site will help.

Learn the Net
http://www.learnthenet.com/english/index.html
Learn the Net specializes in online training products and services for the corporate world. Their guide is well written and up-to-date. It is an excellent source of information for the beginner.

Many of you reading this guide have a lot of experience with computers, while others have little or none. Before proceeding, you should have and be familiar with a few basic resources:
1. computers
2. Web browsers
3. Internet connections

Don't worry if you can't afford your own resources. There are many free or inexpensive options available to you, and we'll do our best to show them to you. The use of computer labs is now a common and even required component of

1

most courses. Also, we're pretty confident that these computers have one of the popular browsers by Netscape or Microsoft and an Internet connection. If you haven't found your campus computer lab yet, then our guess is that you'll find it associated with your campus library. From a beginner's point of view, the only real concern you'll have is learning the basics.

Searching the World

Although many wire-heads consider the Internet to be the largest library on the planet, it doesn't necessarily have the easiest card catalog in the world. In this section, we'll explore techniques for searching the Internet, discuss practices for evaluating the validity of the content you find, discuss online education, explain CD-based Companion Website learning, and review guidelines for citing information within your class assignments. With practice, these skills will help you improve your usage of the Internet.

There is one skill, or rather behavior, that you must adopt in order to maximize your time-to-gain ratio. That is, be aware of "search drift." The Internet is an information jungle and if you wander into it without having a sound idea of why you are there, or if you just wander around without being aware of where you are, then you will get "lost" and waste a great deal of time. Yes, there are times when you will want to play, wander, and have a good time, but consider whether the best time to do that is the night before a test.

Searching

Yahoo! is a good place to begin. It is only one of many resources available on the Internet. It's easy to remember. If you have a chance, log onto the site and follow along as we describe how to use it.

> **Yahoo!:** http://www.yahoo.com
> Yahoo! began as a simple listing of information by category—kind of like a card catalog. As it's grown, it has added the ability to search for specific information—and many, many other features that we encourage you to explore. At the top level of the directory there are several very general categories, but as you move deeper into the directory, notice that the categories become more specific. To find information, you simply choose the most appropriate category at the top level and continue through each successive level until you find what you're looking for (or until you realize you're in the wrong place). Don't be afraid to experiment—it's easy to get lost but also easy to find your way home. Because Yahoo! cross-references among the categories, you'll find that several related categories will lead you to your desired page.

Prepare yourself for a search *before* you jump into one. In the long run, it will save you both time and frustration. Don't be afraid to try some strange approaches for your search strategy. A good technique is to pull out your thesaurus and look up other names for the word. You might be able to find a more common form of the word. Think of everything associated with your question and give each of these subjects a try. You never know what might turn up a gold mine of information.

The following list of resources contain many more helpful tools, tips, and techniques for searching the Internet. If you have specific academic needs, many of these tools are what you'll want to use.

Librarians' Index to the Internet
http://lii.org/
Nueva School Search Strategy Planner
http://www.nueva.pvt.k12.ca.us/~debbie/library/research/
adviceengine.html
NoodleQuest Search Tools
http://www.noodletools.com/noodlequest/

Search Engines

A more direct approach to finding information on the Web is to use a search engine, which is a program that runs a search while you wait for the results. Many search engines can be found on the Web. Some Web search engines are commercial and may charge you a fee to run a search. Search engines are also available for other parts of the Internet: **Archie, Veronica,** and **Jughead** are examples of such search engines.

As mentioned earlier, Yahoo! has a useful search engine. Another search engine that is used frequently is called Lycos (http://www.lycos.com). Google is also a great search engine (http://www.google.com). Lycos is simple to operate but, as with any search tool, it takes practice and patience to master. Take the time now to connect to Lycos, and we'll take it for a test run. When you first see the opening page, you'll notice that it is very complex. But it's an excellent resource, and the instructions on the page will tell you almost everything you need to know. To search, enter a word into the white text-entry box and press the submit button. Lycos will refer back to its database of information and return to you a page of hyperlinked resources to various sites on the Internet that contain your search word.

When you type in a word or category to search, you'll notice that some of your results don't seem to apply to your topic. This is one of the pitfalls of search engines. They are very fast, but they don't think—that is your job. A search using the term "coral reef" is just as likely to turn up a link to Jimmy Buffett's Coral Reefer Band as a link to coral reef research. To perform an effective search, you will need to spend time *before* the search preparing a search strategy. When you do research using an automated tool like a search engine, you can expect many links to be unrelated to your topic of interest—but all in all, search engines are still very powerful tools.

Another type of search service that you'll hear much about is called a meta-search service. This type of service will send your query out to a number of

3

different search engines and then tabulate the results for you. Meta-searches come in many different levels of sophistication and they also generate a large amount of information. If you're not intimidated by volume then give one of them a try.

Here's a meta-search tool that is both fun to use and powerful. Give it a try.
Ask Jeeves: http://www.askjeeves.com

One last word on search engines. These tools don't directly search the Internet. They actually search a database that is derived from the Internet. Here is how it works: Search engines use robots (automated programming tools) that search for and categorize information. This information is placed into a database. It is this database that you search when you use the search engine. Can you think of a potential problem with this system? Unfortunately, the quality of the database depends on the effectiveness of the robot that assembles the database. This is why you should not rely on just one search-engine tool. Use several because what one does not find, another might. You shouldn't have trouble finding other search engines if you don't like the ones we list here. Both of the major browsers now include a basic menu button that will connect you to a large collection of different search engines.

The following resources will help you learn more about searching the Internet.
How to Search the Web from Palomar College
http://daphne.palomar.edu/TGSEARCH
Search Engine Watch
http://searchenginewatch.com
http://searchenginewatch.com/resources/tutorials.html
Search Guide
http://www.searchengineguide.org

4

Chapter 2

Staying in Touch

Although the Internet is sometimes thought of as a flashy, graphically rich waste of time, it began as a tool to enable researchers to communicate between research labs across the United States. If you look at its basic features, the Internet is still a valuable and effective tool for communication. In essence, one goal of the Internet has been to eliminate the hindrance of geography on the free exchange of ideas. Whether it becomes a waste of time or a time-saving tool is entirely up to you. We hope the following ideas will help you make the most of the Internet as a tool for communication and collaboration.

A Mailbox in Cyberspace

An e-mail account is the most basic of methods for planting yourself in the Internet community. Do you have one? Don't worry if you don't. We have a number of simple, inexpensive, and fast solutions you may want to consider.

There are a few options available to you. You may be able to apply for an e-mail account through your college. If your college doesn't provide student e-mail accounts, then e-mail service through an Internet Service Provider (ISP) is a second option. ISPs require you to subscribe (meaning spend money) to acquire their service. The nature of service, hourly or monthly, will depend on your anticipated use. Although you will need to pay a fee for the service, there is an advantage because you can expect help from time to time, which you are not as likely to receive from other options.

Should you wish to pursue this option—and if you have the cash—you can find a national list of ISPs at the following address: http://www.boardwatch.com. Costs average about $20 per month depending on the services that you use. We suggest that you do not sign a long-term contract with an ISP until you are certain that you are happy with the service that particular provider offers. Most providers offer a free trial period before any formal commitment is necessary. Test the system at various times during the day to be certain that sufficient access is provided.

A third option, which is increasing in popularity, is to choose a free e-mail service provided by one of the many online companies. Yes, a free e-mail account with many of the bells and whistles found in a regular e-mail account can be yours for the asking. If you choose a free e-mail service, then read the fine print and understand what it means to you. In most cases, the service is provided to you free because the provider is making its money by selling advertising space to other companies. This is the same way that search engine companies and television stations make their money. In order to read your mail, you have to wade through a few commercials prominently posted on your e-mail reader. An additional condition of these free e-mail accounts is that they will gather information about you in order to customize and target the display of commercials for you. In most cases, this information is used only to target you with commercials, but always read the fine print.

The following are only a few of the more prominent services offering free e-mail and free Internet access in general. Read the fine print in their service agreements, and choose the one that offers you the most. Also, don't be afraid to change services if you're not getting what you expect.

E-Mail Service	Web Address
Hotmail	http://www.hotmail.com
Juno	http://www.juno.com
Netscape	http://webmail.netscape.com
NetZero	http://www.netzero.com
Yahoo!	http://mail.yahoo.com

So, now that you're on your way to your own e-mail account, what are you going to do with it?

Simple Suggestions
If you wish to skip all of the instructions, here are a few suggestions to keep you out of trouble.
- Write down the user ID and password for your account. It's difficult to read your e-mail if you can't get into your account.
- Change your password periodically. Someone stealing your login information could do a number of unscrupulous things with your account and reputation.
- Don't use the same password for all of your accounts. Yes, it is much easier to remember if you do, but it is also much easier for someone else, too.
- Watch out for e-mail viruses. They are common and can unintentionally be passed through attached documents.

E-Mail and Your Instructor
E-mail is becoming a very common and popular way for students and instructors to communicate outside of class. As you progress through college, it is likely that you will have numerous e-mail exchanges with your instructors. The following should help you greatly.
- When communicating with your instructors, use correct spelling, grammar, punctuation, and clarity—just as you would with a carefully crafted letter.
- Most instructors will refrain from sending confidential information through e-mail since one can't guarantee the security of the message. Therefore, it is best not to request confidential information, exam scores, or course grades electronically.

6

- If you are asked to submit assignments electronically, be very careful as to the timing and the format you select.
- Smaller bits of text, such as summaries or project descriptions, can be sent in the body of the message; however, larger documents, including graphs and tables, should be sent as attachments. Your instructor will give you specific instructions about submitting such documents.
- Most instructors will have a mechanism for acknowledging receipt of important documents. If you have not received an acknowledging document, be certain to check by phone or in person with the instructor. It is the student's responsibility to be certain that all assignments are received in an acceptable form.

E-Mail Etiquette

Etiquette is especially important with e-mail communication. When engaged in a conversation, it is likely that you are also communicating information with the inflections in your voice, the expression on your face, and the posture of your body. If you take any or all of these away, there is a greater chance for miscommunication. Here are a few suggestions to help you out in the e-mail world.

- Say what you mean, say it concisely, and say it very carefully—once you've sent it, it is "there" and cannot be retrieved. We have all had to follow-up a vague or hurtful e-mail with explanations or apologies.
- Get to the point—your instructor is probably very busy and will be unwilling to read a tome. If you want to chat then we suggest a pizza.
- Use the subject line—it's a quick way to tell the other person what you want.
- Don't shoot from the hip. Sometimes normally timid people become raging bulls when online.
- Understand the distinction between Reply and Reply All on the menu bar—or you may have just sent your most passionate love-letter to a mailing list.
- Use a "smiley" when you think there is a possibility for misinterpretation—with e-mail, there is no opportunity to convey varied meanings by tone of voice or body language. :-)

This is by no means all there is to know about etiquette on the Net (netiquette) and the ins-and-outs of e-mail, but it's a beginning. Each institution will supply more definite guidelines. Read them and follow them. The following list of URLs should help you find, understand, and use your e-mail to peak efficiency—or at least to maximum entertainment.

A Beginner's Guide to Effective Email by Kaitlin Duck Sherwood
http://www.webfoot.com/advice/email.top.html

Email Etiquette from Air Canada
http://www.acra.ca/mlist/emailetiquette.htm

A Place to Call Home

After setting up an e-mail account, a homepage is the next logical step toward establishing yourself with an Internet presence. Considering the proliferation of personal homepages and the typical merit of their content, you might not realize the advantages that a personal homepage may offer to you. While an e-mail account offers you an identity on the Internet, a homepage offers you a central resource that is mostly under your control. As a student, you are somewhat nomadic and therefore required to work in many different locations throughout the day. A homepage can be an important central resource for your nomadic life. Your homepage could list online reference sites such as search engines, dictionaries, directories, and glossaries; a hyperlinked list of e-mail addresses for your instructors, classmates, and friends; a place where you can post shared information for your study groups; or a place to post class assignments for your instructors. In short, a homepage may be passive in nature but it can be a valuable tool for communication and it can save you a lot of time.

You have three basic options for posting and maintaining a homepage on the Internet. Your college may offer you space to post and maintain a homepage, you can subscribe to an ISP, or you can use a free service. The business model used by free e-mail services is similar to that of companies providing free homepage services. In most cases, these services have a basic format that you can occasionally add to or modify. Read the fine print to make sure you understand the agreement.

The following services enable you to set up a homepage on the Internet. Each of them offers a slightly different service, so spend a bit of time to really evaluate their offerings.

Home Page Service	Web Address
Geocities	http://www.geocities.com/join/
Netscape	http://my.netscape.com/
Yahoo!	http://my.yahoo.com/
NetColony	http://www.netcolony.com

Part of the fun of having a homepage is creating it to reflect your interests and personality. As you begin moving through the Web you'll notice a great variety of homepages. Some of them are not so good but a number are both expressive and functional. As you begin to design your own homepage, remember what you want it to do and say about you.

The following online resource should help you begin building your first homepage. With a quick search of the Internet, you will find a large number of other resources along this line. Be creative and enjoy the experience.

The Bare Bones Guide to HTML by Kevin Werbach
http://werbach.com/barebones/

If this isn't enough then the following sites can give you even more information on Web page design:

Internet.com	http://www.webreference.com
Art and the Zen of Web Sites	http://www.tlc-systems.com/webtips.html
Creating Killer Sites	http://www.killersites.com
WebDeveloper.com	http://www.webdeveloper.com
Web Building	http://builder.com
Web Monkey	htttp://www.hotwired.lycos.com/webmonkey

The Need for Plug-ins

Plug-ins are software programs that extend the capabilities of a particular browser in some specific manner, giving you the opportunity to play audio samples or view movies from within the browser. Such plug-ins are usually "cross platform" in that they can be used on Macintosh or Windows systems. Below are some examples of important and popular plug-ins that you'll probably need to view the more interactive websites.

* *Flash Player* by Macromedia—This plug-in will allow you to view animation and interactive content through your browser. This interactive content includes cartoons and games from leading-edge companies like Comedy Central, Sony, and Disney. You'll also need this plug-in to view many of the science animations being developed for your books. (http://www.flash.com)

* *Shockwave* by Macromedia—This is the industry standard for delivering interactive multimedia, graphics, and streaming audio on the Web. Major companies like CNN, Capitol Records, and Paramount use Shockwave as their delivery system. (http://www.macromedia.com/shockwave/download/)

* *RealPlayer* by RealNetworks—This plug-in allows you to play audio, video, animation, and multimedia presentations on the Web. RealPlayer Plus gives sharp pictures and audio for RealAudio and RealVideo. Many popular radio and television shows are available on the Web if you have this plug-in. (http://www.realplayer.com)

* *QuickTime* by Apple Computer—This plug-in allows you to play audio/video productions and is commonly included on CDs. It is extremely common and is typically preinstalled in the recent versions of both major browsers. Upgrades are very frequent so you can always download the newest version at Apple's website. (http://www.apple.com/quicktime/download/)

If you wish to download these or other plug-ins, then you can go directly to the company that makes them or to the download gallery of the browser that you use. Both major browsers provide a listing of plug-ins by category for your access. Simply download the one you want and then follow the installation instructions.

A Calendar of Events

The final step in our project to help you stay in touch with your classes, friends, and family is to make you aware of the help that a calendar program can lend. By now, it should be obvious to you that your life is not going to get less complicated. Having a tool to help you schedule your time and remember important events will be a distinct asset. Developing a routine to organize your life is the first and best step to take. The second step is to find a tool to help you remember your reading and homework assignments, library time, class schedules, exams, study-group meetings, and office hours for your instructors—in addition to all of your personal commitments.

In addition to offering you free e-mail, Yahoo!, Netscape, and many other companies offer a free online calendar service. The service is free—provided you register. By now you should be familiar with the model. The service is free to you, but you'll need to provide them with some basic personal information and you will need to endure the targeted commercials embedded in your calendar viewer. With this service, you will be able to populate a calendar with events that are important to you. Your calendar of events is viewable by day, week, month, or year. It will contain both a "To Do" list and a regular daily schedule. One of the potentially valuable resources is that of scheduled e-mail notes to remind you of important events. Never again do you need to suffer those nightmares of forgetting an exam. However, you do need to make the commitment to maintain the accuracy of your calendar. Additionally, if you know basic HTML, you can schedule events to include hyperlinks. These could be to references sites, assignments posted by your instructors, or to resources posted on the Companion Website for your textbook. Essentially, your calendar can be completely linked to the Internet.

Parting advice: Remember that you have the power of the purse; therefore, always look for the least expensive option, read and understand an agreement before you sign it, and enjoy your journey.

Something Called Privacy

The Internet has been moving over the last few years to increase the level of personalization that users experience when they browse. This personalization can be both good and bad—with increased personalization there is also less privacy. Information about you, and your viewing, and possibly purchase habits, is a commodity that companies want. If your likes and dislikes are known, then it is much easier to specifically market a product to you. For example, if I notice that you always come into my record store and browse through the Blues section, it is unlikely that I'll sell you something from the Sex Pistols. But I have a better chance of pulling you in if I run a special on B.B. King. Some companies are in the business of providing information about you and they collect this information on the Web. Read the fine print before you sign up, register, or provide your personal information to anyone or anything on the Web.

There are plenty of powerful people worried about privacy on the Internet, so we are not alone. The following Web addresses are for some of the many organizations that have dedicated themselves to securing and lobbying for Internet privacy. It might be a helpful exercise to make a visit to their site and learn more about the situation.

Privacy Organization	Web Address
Electronic Privacy Information Center	http://epic.org
Electronic Frontier Foundation	http://www.eff.org
Center for Democracy & Technology's Operation	http://opt-out.cdt.org
Junkbusters	http://www.junkbusters.com

DoubleClick is one of the leading companies that gathers information about people and their browsing habits. If you want to learn more about what they do and how to remove yourself from their observation, visit their site.

DoubleClick
http://www.doubleclick.net/privacy_policy/privacy.htm

We're not trying to create a sense of mistrust about using the Internet. We don't want you to confuse the Internet with the *X-Files*. The great majority of times that you are asked to supply information on the Internet, it is safe to do so and is meant to help the requester more fully service your needs, but it pays to be informed about the issues involved.

Chapter 3

Using ContentSelect to Locate Information

ContentSelect is an archive of scholarly peer-reviewed journals and general interest periodicals. Thousands of articles from popular publications and prestigious academic journals can be instantly accessed in a multitude of ways using ContentSelect's search engine. Titles are chosen to reflect multiple perspectives in a wide range of topics; specific content areas include Anthropology, Communications, Computer Science, Criminal Justice, Education, Finance, Economics, History, Marketing and Management, Medical Sciences, Political Science, Psychology, Social Work, and Sociology.

Of course, ContentSelect is not a substitute for evaluation: careful research studies sometimes contradict one another, and even authorities disagree. However, while many sources on the Internet may present questionable data or rely on dubious authorities to draw conclusions, ContentSelect provides a wealth of professionally reviewed information that you can search and evaluate with confidence. People recognized as experts in the field have already subjected such peer-reviewed writing, like that in academic journals, to rigorous analysis.

Although there are a number of articles targeted at a general audience in ContentSelect, it is important to remember that the academic articles are written for a professional audience and are generally very narrowly focused on a specific topic. These articles might use special terminology not readily recognizable by the general reader.

While the specialization of these articles makes them harder to read, it also makes them especially valuable as sources of primary information, or original results discovered or conceived by a researcher. You may wish to pay special attention to the abstract and discussion before reading the rest of the paper to get a general idea of what the author intends her paper to say. The abstract presents a concise summary of the paper's purpose; the discussion section at the end of the paper reviews these purposes and emphasizes the researcher's findings and their implications.

Registering for ContentSelect

Before you can access articles on ContentSelect, you must first have a valid login and password.

To register for a login and password, click New Users at the ContentSelect home page (http://contentselect.pearsoncmg.com/) and enter the six-word access code included with your textbook into the dialog box. The site is best viewed at 1024 x 768 resolution, so you may wish to change your monitor to this setting before opening the page. After selecting the New User button on the same page, click Next. Then, follow the on-screen instructions to complete the registration process.

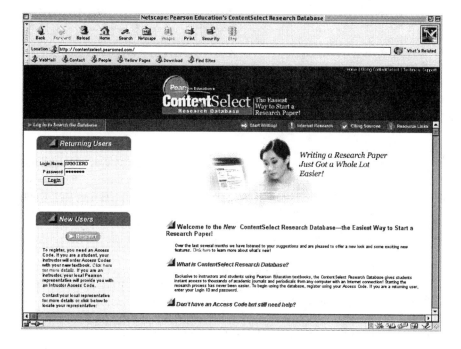

How to Use ContentSelect

Remember: the site is best viewed at 1024 x 768 resolution, so you may wish to change your monitor settings appropriately.

After typing your login and password to ContentSelect in the fields under Returning Users, click Login to enter the database. You should see a screen like the one pictured as follows. Each of the titles on this screen is a ContentSelect database that you can search. Clicking on the title of the database shows you the list of journals in each database.

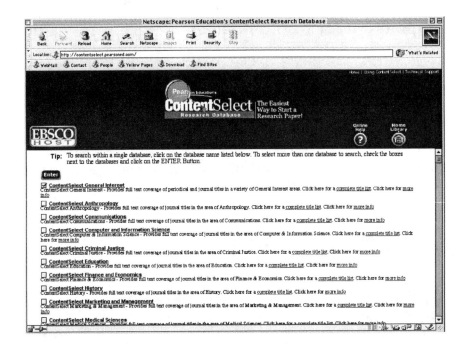

If you'd like to search one of these databases, click on the check box next to the title. (You can click on as many of these check boxes as you want – they will all be searched in the search window. Note that you can return to this window later if you want to add or remove databases from the list you want to search.) Once you've clicked all the databases you'd like to search, press the "Enter" button at the top (or bottom) of the page to go to the search window.

In the search window, the one shown in the picture that follows, you can type a word or phrase into the Find box as shown and click Search to access articles matching those keywords. Clicking on one of the buttons below the Find box changes how ContentSelect will search the database; instructions that appear when clicking on these buttons will tell you how each search differs. You can also find out how to use these functions, and other functions of ContentSelect's search tool, in the "Search Tips" section. Note that you can start a new search at any time with the "New Search" button at the top of the page. Similarly, the "Change Databases" button returns you to the list of databases and allows you to select new ones to search.

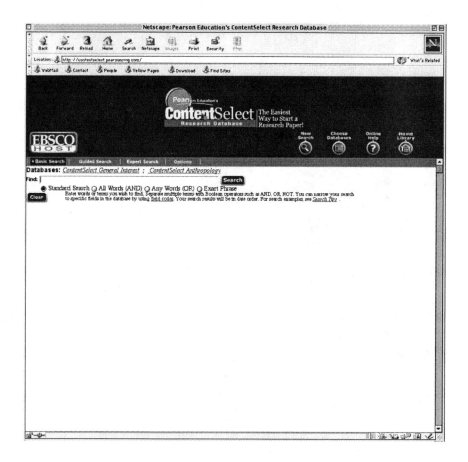

After clicking Search, you'll be presented with a list of articles that matched your keywords (such as the one in the illustration that follows). If none of the articles matched your keywords, you will be returned to the search window to try other keywords. Clicking on the title of an article opens a window with the article and a full citation. You can read this article, mark it for later printing, e-mail it to someone, save it to your disk, return to your original list of search results, or refine your search to reduce the number of articles returned by clicking on the matching buttons at the top or bottom of the article page and following the instructions.

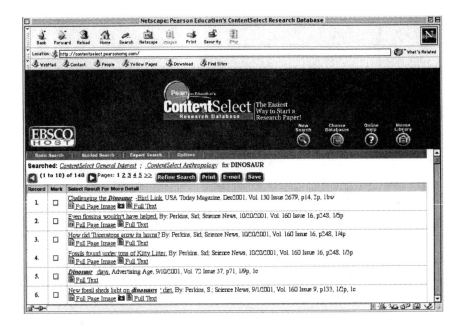

ContentSelect Search Tips

At the top of the Search window, there are four tabs: *Basic Search*, *Guided Search*, *Expert Search*, and *Options*. This section will teach you how to use each of these tools to refine your search to find articles that closely pertain to the subject that you are researching.

Basic Search

The *Basic Search* option allows you to construct a Keyword or Boolean search. The basic search window is the one that comes up when you enter ContentSelect (and that was depicted before). Use the operators *and*, *or*, and *not* to create a very broad search or a very narrow search. By default, the results of a Boolean search are displayed in descending date order, with the most recent article displayed first.

And combines search terms so that each result contains all of the terms. For instance, typing *Spain and France* returns articles that contain both of these words. *Or* combines search terms so that each result contains *at least one* of the terms. Typing *hockey or football* would return results containing either word. *Not* excludes terms so that each result *does not contain* the term that follows the *not* operator. A search for *cell not prison* would return articles that contained the word *cell* and that also did not have the word *prison*.

In addition to typing Boolean search operators like *and, or,* and *not* into the Find window, you can select them using the appropriate buttons. Clicking the *And* button, for instance, makes the search treat every word in the Find window as though it had *and* after it. Thus, typing in *evolution psychology* with *And* selected is like typing in *evolution and psychology*.

Stop Words

Note that in all your searches, words like *or*, *the*, and *for* are ignored. These ignored words are called stop words. So, if you type in *Emperor of Rome*, ContentSelect will search for a phrase with *Emperor* first, *Rome* last, and <u>any</u> word in the place of the ignored words in between. Searching *Emperor of Rome* will return articles with keywords *Emperor for Rome*, *Emperor the Rome*, *Emperor after Rome*, et cetera.

Quotation Marks

Placing a phrase in quotation marks makes ContentSelect search for that exact phrase; Boolean operators and stop words are ignored if they are in quotation marks. Searching for *Pride and Prejudice* returns results containing that exact phrase only; <u>not</u> results with the keywords *pride* and *prejudice*.

Punctuation

When a phrase containing punctuation is typed into ContentSelect, results are returned with keywords both containing and not containing the punctuation. Therefore, typing in *Printers: Inkjet* returns articles containing *Printers: Inkjet* and *Printers Inkjet*.

Wildcard (?) and Truncation (*) Symbols

When performing a search, you can use the symbols *?* and * to greatly broaden the results that you receive.

Typing in the wildcard operator returns words with any letter in place of the wildcard. For instance, searching *p?t* would return articles containing the words *pat*, *pot*, *pet*, *pit*, and *put*.

If you use the truncation symbol in a search, ContentSelect will return articles with any variation of the root word you typed in. For instance, if you searched for *writ**, you would receive results for *writer, writing,* and *written.*

Proximity Searches

Use this handy function to search for groups of words that you think will not necessarily be close to one another. Let's say, for instance, that you want to find articles on the *United States Constitution*, but that you don't think that these words will necessarily be found near one another.

Near Operator (N)

Searching for *"United States" N4 Constitution* will find articles with the phrase *United States* appearing no more than four words <u>before</u> o r <u>after</u> the word *Constitution*. Changing the number in front of the operator changes the number of words that ContentSelect will allow to be in between the two phrases; *"United States" N8 Constitution* would allow *United States* to come up to eight words before or after *Constitution*.

Within Operator (W)

Searching for *"United States" W4 Constitution* will find articles with the phrase *United States* appearing no more than four words <u>before</u>, <u>not</u> <u>after</u>, the word *Constitution*. The W operator, unlike the N operator, is sensitive to the order in which the words are typed. Changing the number in front of the operator changes the number of words that ContentSelect will allow to be in between the two phrases; *"United States" W8 Constitution* would allow *United States* to come up to eight words before, but not after, *Constitution.*

Guided Search

The *Guided Search* option performs a more specific Boolean search; that is, you can use all of the options that we used in the *Basic Search,* but guided searches have additional features with which to tailor the search.

With guided searches, you can enter a word or phrase into each field and tell ContentSelect to look for that word or phrase in a certain part of the article only. The dialog box next to each field has a number of different parts of the article that are searchable. For instance, you might want to tell ContentSelect to look for articles written by anyone with the last name *Faulkner*; to do so, you could perform a guided search for *Faulkner* with *AU Author* selected in the corresponding dialog box. A sample search is shown in the picture that follows. Searchable fields include Author, Title, Abstract, and Journal Title, among others.

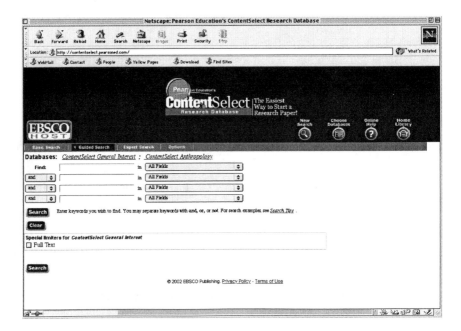

To put Boolean operators between the words/phrases that you've entered in the various fields, use the corresponding dialog boxes to the left of each entry field. Note that if you have more than one phrase entered in the guided search, you must specify which Boolean operator is to be used. The default setting is for *and* to be placed between each word.

Expert Search

Expert searching combines elements of *Basic* and *Guided* searching, along with a few new options that make searching more flexible.

The expert search window is depicted as follows. Expert searching is based on using different field codes to specify precisely what you'd like ContentSelect to look for. These codes can be viewed by clicking the Field Codes link.

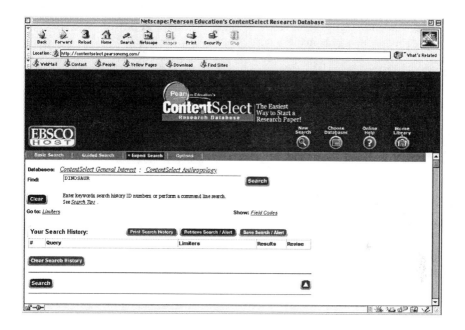

To search, combine field codes with desired keywords to tell ContentSelect precisely what kind of article that you're looking for. For instance, if you're looking for an article published in 1999 in the *Journal of Higher Education*, you'd type in *YP 1999 and SO Journal of Higher Education.* YP is the field code for year published, and SO is the code for journal title.

You can use parentheses to tell ContentSelect which parts of the search are relatively more important than other parts. For instance, typing in *(YP 1999 or TI Learning) and SO Journal of Higher Education* tells ContentSelect to first find the set of all articles that were published in 1999 or have *Learning* in the title, then return all the articles in this set that are also published in the *Journal of Higher Education.* Changing the parentheses slightly, however, greatly modifies the search. *YP 1999 or (TI Learning and SO Journal of Higher Education)* tells ContentSelect to first find all the articles that are published in the *Journal of Higher Education* and that have *Learning* in the title, and then return all the articles in this set plus all the articles published in 1999.

Past searches in *Expert Search* mode can also be combined. Say that you have two past searches, labeled S1 and S2. These searches are shown in the Your Search History list beneath the Find field. To combine these searches, type *S1 and S2* into the Find field: ContentSelect will report back all of the articles that were present in both searches.

All of the Boolean operators can be used with the field codes and past search codes to create a very focused search. Because the codes and structure of an entry are a bit difficult to manage, however, you may wish to refer frequently to the Field Codes and Search Tips links on the *Expert Search* page.

Using ContentSelect to find strong primary material can provide you with the basis for recognizing the inadequacies in other Web-based sources.

Chapter 4

Is More Information a Plus? It Can Be

In your career as a student and eventually as a professional, you will spend a great deal of time using the Internet to communicate and find information. But can you trust the information you find? We want to give you hints about how to judge the information you receive from the Internet. *It's not more information you need, but the ability to evaluate what you already have.*

This guide explains what to do after you have retrieved information from a website. Should you believe the information? Should you rely on it? Should you use it as a basis for your statements when you speak or write?

The Internet contains approximately 800 million publicly-indexed Web pages,[1] providing access to a vast amount of information with a few clicks of a mouse. You can: make reservations to travel to Italy; read reviews and decide which books to read or movies to see; check out college descriptions of campuses and programs; read research studies and articles about topics ranging from new medical treatments to the status of women in Saudi Arabia; and enter digital libraries without leaving your chair.

Having so much information readily available is exciting. Whatever the topic, you can probably find information about it. For example, suppose that your political science professor has asked you to research the development of the Federal Reserve system. You do a quick search, and come across a website with the following information:

> The Federal Reserve, the central bank of the United States, was founded by Congress in 1913 to provide the nation with a safer, more flexible, and more stable monetary and financial system. (http://www. federalreserve.gov)

You jot down some notes from this website, and then locate another relevant site, which provides the following information:

> The Federal Reserve is neither Federal nor a Reserve. It is a private Cashist Cartel. It is totally owned and totally controlled by the International Banksters. The Fed creates "currency" out of thin air and then loans it back to you, through the Federal Government, at "interest"

---

[1] Steve Lawrence and C. Lee Giles, "Accessibility of Information on the Web," *Nature* (1999).

for the life of each note. It buys these notes which you call dollars for the cost of printing and paper. That's about 2 cents for a one, a fifty or a one hundred dollar bill. It doesn't matter the price is always the same. For them, the price is about 2 cents per note regardless of the denomination. And that's a hefty profit. It costs us face value plus interest for the life of the note. A "Note," by the way is an obligation to pay. And who do you pay? The Federal Reserve one way or another gets theirs. And you, one way or another gets screwed. That's the size of it.

But there is a problem here. Both of these sites can't be correct. Is the Federal Reserve an instrument of the American national government or is it a tool by which "International Banksters" rob the world? Which site should we believe?

Is More Information Better Information?

The Internet is deceptive. Because it is easy to find large amounts of information, we tend to feel excited about it. But if we confuse quantity with quality, we will overlook the need to process all that information. We must choose which facts to accept and which ones to set aside as undependable.

You may have used a search engine such as Yahoo, Infoseek, or Excite. Each of these indexes approximately 16% of the 800 million pages indexed on the Internet.[2] Thus, if you conduct a search with Yahoo and another search with Excite, you will probably find two different sets of Web pages. How do we know which ones offer accurate information?

Let's return to the example of the Federal Reserve research project. If we were to search for more information on the history of this agency--a good place to start when looking for the historical development--we could check any of the following websites:

- **Board of Governors of the Federal Reserve System**
  (http://www.federalreserve.gov)
- **Woodrow Federal Reserve Bank of Minneapolis**
  (http://woodrow.mpls.frb.fed.us/info/policy/)
- **Early History and Developments of Bank and Branching Regulation**
  (http://cber.nlu.edu/DBR/Z2-5.htm)
- **Federal Reserve Bank of San Francisco**
  (http://www.frbsf.org/federalreserve)

But we don't know whether the information on our topic from any of these sites is dependable. Furthermore, we probably wouldn't take the time to look at all of these websites. In fact, we might look at only one of the two discussed earlier. Suppose that you only looked at the site that suggested that the Federal Reserve

---

[2] Ibid.

was unconstitutional and wholly corrupt. You would probably simply accept the information and begin to write your paper.

This example highlights an important danger of the Internet. How do you know that the author of the website is providing accurate information?

Assuming That Information Is Dependable

When we read something on the Internet, we may assume that the information is accurate and dependable. However, remember that anyone can create a Web page and put it on the Internet. The author of a Web page might have little or no knowledge about the topic. Thus, when you search for information about the history of the Federal Reserve, you might find a page written by someone who took one economics or political science class in college and another written by a professor of the subject. The fact that a page is on the Internet says nothing about the quality of the information there.

The authors of these sites often want you to believe that you have found the truth on their pages. They state their information without the ordinary cautions that reputable experts would provide. Therefore, it is very easy to find highly-biased information on the Internet.

If you do not question the information provided on a website, you risk accepting flawed information. In the Federal Reserve example, you might have gotten a failing grade on your paper had you trusted the site written by the person with only one class in political science. You need to question that information. Healthy doubt is positive self-defense.

You Control Information; It Doesn't Control You

If you assume that information on the Internet is dependable, you become a passive recipient of that information. When you passively use information, it determines how you react. For example, suppose that you are exploring on the Internet and you read the following statement:

> True social harmony grows naturally out of solidarity of interests. In a society where those who always work never have anything, while those who never work enjoy everything, solidarity of interests is non-existent; hence social harmony is but a myth. The only way organized authority meets this grave situation is by extending still greater privileges to those who have already monopolized the earth, and by still further enslaving the disinherited masses. Thus the entire arsenal of government--laws, police, soldiers, the courts, legislatures, prisons--is strenuously engaged in harmonizing the most antagonistic elements in society.

If you passively accepted this information, you would probably have a sense of mistrust or even hostility towards our political system. The information is shaping your behavior.

Certainly, some of the information on the Internet is dependable. To determine which information is dependable, you must actively reflect about whether you should accept each item as correct. In other words, you must take control of the information and use it only if it meets your standards.

If it does not meet those standards, you will want to keep looking. You might find additional information that will lead you to accept a modified version of the original information. The point is that YOU decide whether information is worthwhile. Consequently, you are in control of the information, and you therefore control your behavior.

As just noted, one way to question information you find on the Internet is to look for additional information. For example, you might want to search for a site that offers conflicting information. (Authors rarely offer links to sites that disagree with theirs.) When you search for conflicting information you are acting on the information, instead of letting the person who created a website control you.

When websites disagree, what should you do? You might begin to feel as though you will never be able to make decisions because there is so much contradictory information. Try not to feel overwhelmed; recognize your confusion is normal. You will soon learn tools that can help you decide which information to accept. For now, it is important to realize that actively searching for conflicting information is one way to question information offered on a Web page.

The Need for Critical Thinking

As stated earlier, when you assume that information is dependable, you risk accepting flawed information. What are the consequences of accepting and using flawed information? First, you might include flawed information in a paper. If your teacher is aware of this, you might get a lower grade. Second, you might use flawed information when making choices as a consumer. This could hurt you financially. For example, suppose that a website reports that a certain stock is sure to provide high returns. Your grandparents use their life savings to buy this stock. However, the information on the website is incorrect, and your grandparents lose all their money.

To control the information you encounter on the Internet, you must actively question it. Looking for additional information is one tool for doing so. This book provides several other tools that will enable you to think critically about information on the Internet.

Critical thinking is the process of using a set of critical questions to evaluate information. In the following chapters, you will learn a set of questions that you can use in deciding whether you should accept or reject the information you encounter on the Internet. Asking these questions is a powerful strategy for distinguishing clear thinking from sloppy thinking. You are not using critical thinking to find "right" or "wrong" information regarding an issue. Instead, you will be using critical questions to find accurate or reasonable information.

Chapter 4

What Argument Does the Site Make?

A constant question that comes up in political philosophy is whether equality of condition is more important than equality of opportunity. Suppose that, in the course of reading about this dilemma, you find a website that says the following:

> Equality of opportunity is impossible to achieve without equality of condition. Unless we all start from the same point, we can never be sure whether someone had an unfair advantage over someone else in life. How can we claim that the person who fails has done so because she deserves to if she doesn't have an equal playing field?

After searching a few more sites, you may find another site with this conflicting information:

> Trying to impose equality of condition only makes us all worse off in the end. There's less to go around when there's no incentive to get better, and so everyone's portion is smaller than the smallest portion was before: it's positively unjust.

These two Web pages come to different conclusions about whether equality of condition is more just than equality of opportunity. So, how do we come to a well-informed decision? With whom should we agree?

In Chapter 1 you learned the importance of questioning the information you find on the Internet. But what information should you question? You might locate a website that has six pages of text. You don't have the time or the interest to question every sentence in those six pages. But it isn't necessary to question every sentence. Instead, you need to identify the author's argument and apply critical thinking skills to it.

An argument is an author's conclusion plus the reasons offered in support of that conclusion. Thus, when we say that critical thinking is an evaluation of an argument, we mean that it is an evaluation of the conclusion and the reasons for it. Let's break down that definition into its components.

Identifying the Conclusion

A *conclusion* is the point that the author wants you to accept. It is generally the author's opinion, and his or her reason for trying to communicate with you is to share that opinion. To identify the conclusion, you ask, What is the main point?

Identifying the conclusion of a passage is an extremely important, yet somewhat difficult, task.

Here are some hints for finding the conclusion:

- When reading a passage, you should repeatedly thing to yourself: What is the author's main point? What idea or position does she want to accept?
- You will often find a conclusion at the beginning or end of a passage. While you should think about the author's main point while you are reading the whole passage, focus on the first and last paragraphs.
- Look for ideas that seem to be defending, or arguing for, other ideas. The ideas being supported will be conclusions.
- Look for the following words that tell us that a conclusion is on the way: *as a result, consequently, hence, in conclusion,* and *in short.*

You might already happen to agree with an author's conclusion. However, you need to set aside your own views momentarily. Your emotional attachment to an idea is not a good basis for accepting or rejecting an author's position. Before you decide to accept a conclusion, you need to identify the reasons offered in support of that conclusion. Let's practice identifying the conclusion of a passage that you might find at a website:

To justify giving privileges or exemptions or subsidies to some particular group in society, the benefit of doing so for society at large must first be shown. With heterosexual marriage, the case is clear enough. Heterosexual marriage is a matter of genuine social interest because the family is essential to society's reproduction. The crux of my argument, in other words, was that married couples receive the benefits they do not because the state is interested in promoting romantic love or because the Bible says so or because of the influence of special interest groups but rather because the next generation is something that is and should be of interest to all of us. And, by definition, this is not a case that can be made for homosexual unions. To that degree, the attempt to turn the question of domestic partnership into a debate about fairness falls flat.

The author's main point--the conclusion--is that as heterosexuals are more valuable to society than homosexuals they should enjoy more civil rights. The author doesn't use those exact words. However, she tries to convince you that only those relationships which have the potential for procreation should receive legal recognition. You have learned how to identify part of an argument. Now, let's look at the second part: the reasons.

Identifying the Reasons

A *reason* is an explanation for why we should accept a certain conclusion. It answers the question, Why? Reasons establish the credibility of the conclusion. We decide whether to reject or accept a conclusion based on the reasons.

Many types of ideas can be reasons. Reasons can be personal testimonials, research findings, beliefs, or any other statements that offer support for a conclusion. Think of reasons as sawhorses that support a piece of wood (the conclusion). Without the sawhorses, the board would fall. Similarly, without good reasons a conclusion will fall. Your identification and evaluation of reasons will largely determine whether you accept the author's conclusion.

Suppose that an author concludes that parents should carefully monitor their children's use of the Internet. You want to find out why the author came to that conclusion. To find the reasons offered, ask, *Why* should parents monitor their kids' Internet exploration?

When you identify reasons, you need to identify anything the author offers to support her conclusion. For now, we are not concerned with the *quality* of the reasons. You might think that some of the reasons the author provides are pretty poor. However, if the author believes that something is a reason, you must identify it as such. You will be able to evaluate that reason *after* you have completely identified the argument.

In the same way that there are certain words that suggest that a conclusion is coming, there are also words that suggest that the author is offering a reason. The best reason indicator word is *because*.

Other Reason Indicator Words

Also, as a result of, because, first . . . second, for example, for one thing.

Where Do I Find Arguments?

You can find arguments everywhere. When you listen to television commercials, talk with friends, or read almost anything on the Internet, you will find that someone is presenting an argument. That person is trying to persuade you of something. Remember, however, that a belief or opinion presented without reasons is not an argument. Arguments include both a conclusion and reasons supporting it.

Let's practice identifying the argument of a passage you might find on the Web:

> The recent murder of a homosexual college student in Wyoming has sparked predictable cries for the enactment of so-called "hate crimes" legislation. Proposals for such legislation would implement an additional penalty for crimes that seem motivated by intolerance for certain groups.
>
> The most obvious problem with the proposed legislation is surely the absurdity of distinguishing "hate crimes" from other crimes. Should we classify all other criminal acts as "love crimes"? Would having one's family brutally murdered for plain old reasons like money or sadism be somehow less morally grave than a murder motivated by intolerance of homosexuals

or some other politically incorrect sentiment? Such is the unavoidable logic of hate crimes legislation.

For the assumption of hate crimes legislation is that there are more serious crimes out there than murder, or the taking of human life. This assumption seems an all-too-accurate reflection of contemporary liberalism. In an age where suicide of the infirm and elderly, and abortion even very late in the pregnancy, becomes more common, it ought to be no surprise that taking human life seems somehow insufficiently criminal. For liberals to really get their back up about an offense, it must go beyond mere murder and rise to the level of "intolerance."

Conclusion: The solution for criminal behavior is not more laws but tougher enforcement.

Why does the author believe that hate crimes legislation is redundant? Now you are trying to identify the reasons he offers in support of his conclusion. Remember, we are looking for statements that answer the question: "Are some crimes more abhorrent than others?"

Reason: All crime victims are deserving of equal justice.

The author of this passage told us that those that society must be tough on all criminals regardless of their motives. But why is this important? The author later explains why. He offers reasons to support this reason.

Supporting Reason: Contemporary liberals are using hate crime legislation to create a hierarchy of victims, thus giving a priority to crimes against homosexuals.

You have now identified the argument made by the author. You identified the conclusion the author offered as well as the reasons he provided in support of his conclusion. Now what? At this time, all you should be doing is learning to identify arguments. You will soon learn how to use critical questions to determine the value of the information. But before you can do any kind of evaluation, you need to make sure that you have correctly identified the author's argument. The next chapter will build on the ability to identify the arguments presented on websites. Its purpose is to sensitize you to the importance of the source of the information on a site.

Chapter 6

What Is the Source of the Information?

While searching the Internet, you come across this information on a website:

> Many arguments for speech restrictions deny that hateful speech is protected by the Constitution. Such arguments are based on the fact that hate speech does not advance the spirit of free speech. An essay written by judge and lawyer Simon Rifkind emphasizes this point. Fighting words are unprotected because they do not advance the civil discourse, which the First Amendment is designed to promote, Rifkind said. A university is a very special community. Speech which is not civil is at odds with the purpose of the campus.

But after you bookmark this site, you find another site about freedom of speech that presents you with this conflicting information:

> Free speech is protected under our Constitution. The First Amendment protects our speech—even if it is offensive. Adopting speech codes is the same thing as censorship, and this is in violation of the Constitution.

How much should college students be allowed to say on campus? When, if ever, is speech not protected by the Constitution? Is hate speech protected by the Constitution? College administrators throughout the country are heavily debating these issues. Because of this, many Web pages have important things to say about this issue. However, as we said in Chapter 1, it is rare to find a site that presents multiple views on an issue. If we want to find different views, we must go out and find them.

The Importance of the Information Provider

Web pages originate from diverse sources, and the quality of the information they provide varies greatly. Some are much more objective, accurate, comprehensive, and up-to-date than others. Therefore, you should rely much more on some sources than on others.

Variability in the quality of sources is not unique to the Web. It is also characteristic of more traditional sources of information, such as newspapers, television, and magazines. We know, for example, that we ought to pay more attention to claims made in *The New York Times* than to those made in the *National Enquirer*. In such cases, however, we can usually determine pretty easily just what the source is. The source of information and the credibility of that source are much harder to discern on the Internet. Fewer and less obvious clues are available, and there are no accepted standards for presenting material online. Thus, some websites can be trusted much more than others. The first critical-thinking question we need to ask about a Web page is: *What is the source and what do we know about it?*

Differences Among Sources of Information

Sources of information vary in many ways. In some cases we can determine a great deal about the source; in others, very little information about the source is provided. The best websites provide extensive information. Among the things you want to know about a source are: its *motives*, its *content quality*, and its *record of past performance*.

Motives

Websites exist because someone wants them there, not because any independent judge has determined them worthy of inclusion. Their motives and purposes vary greatly, and these differences greatly affect the quality of the information. You therefore need to ask, What is the major motivation behind this site? Is it to inform, to persuade, to sell, to entertain, or to accomplish something else? Knowing the motives behind the site's creation helps you better judge its content. Knowing its motives should also remind you to ask, What is not being said?

To determine the likely motives of website sponsors, you need to ask who sponsored the site and what they say about themselves. Sites vary greatly in how clear and accessible they make this information. Try to obtain the following kinds of information about the site's sponsor:
- The name of the organization or individual responsible for the site.
- Links to additional information about the organization or individual responsible.
- A clear statement of the site's goals.
- A clear indication of any sponsors of the site and whether they are profit or nonprofit. For example, the statement "Funded by the National Institute of Mental Health" clearly indicates a nonprofit sponsor.
- A link to the homepage of the site.
- Links to other important information related to the site, such as a table of contents or bibliographies.

Once you have a good sense of the website sponsor, you should ask: What are the likely motives of the source? Some common motives are:
- To inform
- To advocate

- To sell
- To provide news
- To express individual opinions
- Mixed motives

Let us take a closer look at each of these.

To Inform

The purpose of many websites is to present information relevant to a particular topic. Online library sources and government agencies, for example, are informational. These are likely to be the least biased sources. Many URL addresses that end in **.edu** or **.gov** tend to be informational sources because they are sponsored by educational institutions or by government agencies. Examples of materials found on informational pages include:
- Government statistics
- Information about careers
- Research results
- Directories of businesses

Each of the following sites is primarily informational:
> http://lcweb.loc.gov (Library of Congress)
> http://www.epa.gov (U.S. Environmental Protection Agency)
> http://www.ukans.edu/history/vl/ (History Index)
> http://www.utm.edu/research/iep (The Internet Encyclopedia of Philosophy)
> http://www.doc.gov (U.S. Department of Commerce)

To Advocate

An advocacy page is sponsored by an organization or individual that seeks to influence the opinions of those who access the site. Its purpose is to persuade you. Such pages therefore reflect strong biases, which you need to identify in judging the quality of the information.

Advocacy URL addresses often end in **.org** if they are sponsored by a nonprofit organization. Political parties and self-help groups are examples of advocacy organizations. The following clues suggest an advocacy motivation:
- Seeking of financial donations
- Promotion of a cause
- Efforts to recruit members to an organization
- Provision of ways for like-minded people to pursue further contact

Each of the following is an advocacy site:
> http://www.plannedparenthood.org (Planned Parenthood)
> http://www.nra.org (National Rifle Association)
> http://www.now.org (National Organization for Women)
> http://www.cc.org (Christian Coalition)
> http://aclu.org (American Civil Liberties Union)

To Sell

The primary purpose of many sources is to promote or sell products or services. Thus, you need to be especially alert to biases in information provided by such sites. Virtually everything that is sold in stores is now sold on the Web, including books, appliances, drugs, and clothing. URL addresses whose purpose is to sell often end in **.com**. Following are examples of sites whose main motivation is to sell:

> http://www.amazon.com
> http://www.ebay.com
> http://www.cdnow.com
> http://www.gap.com
> http://www.circuitcity.com

To Provide News

The primary purpose of many websites is to provide current information on diverse issues. Some such sites are simply postings of news from traditional print sources such as *The New York Times, USA Today, Newsweek*, and *Time*. The purpose of some news sites (e.g., Slate.com and Salon.com) is to try to integrate the information from multiple news sites. Examples of news sites include the following:

> http://www.nytimes.com (*New York Times*)
> http://www.usatoday.com (*USA Today*)
> http://www.newsweek.com (*Newsweek*)
> http://www.wsj.com (The Wall Street Journal)

To Express Individual Opinions

Many people create a website as a way to express themselves. They may want to express personal ideas—works of art or poetry, for example—or to pursue hobbies. Some site creators enjoy expressing provocative criticism of existing institutions. Some simply want to "blow their own horn." Personal opinion Web pages are highly diverse and are likely to be very biased. Find out as much as you can about the person behind the site to decide how much attention you should pay to the opinions expressed. Examples of such sites include:

> http://hometown.aol.com/abtrbng/index.htm
> http://www.geocities.com/athens/troy/9087/mlk/mlkdiscuss.htm
> http://members.aol.com/runes3/hate.htm

Mixed Motives

Websites often reflect multiple motives. Be especially alert to sites that suggest one motive (such as informing) but actually reflect other important motives (such as selling). For example, sites that combine the information and selling motives are likely to be less objective than those whose sole motive is to provide information. Another common practice is to make a website look as though it is informing when in fact it is also advocating.

You need to be alert to any motives that bias information on a website. Pay particular attention to the role of advertising and sponsors. Try to determine whether they might be influencing the content of a site. For example, if you are seeking information for a paper on gun control, you should be suspicious of sites sponsored by the National Rifle Association and sites advertising guns, as well as sites sponsored by anti-gun groups.

Noting who is advertising on a website provides you important clues to possible biases. Also, when accessing sites that look like information sites, check the backgrounds of contributors to that site. Do they reflect particular political biases? Are they associated with organizations noted for advocating particular points of view? This information is essential for determining the credibility of the source.

Content Quality

The quality of information available at websites varies greatly. Sometimes you find "garbage," at other times "gold." You need to ask several questions to assess the quality of information at a site. The most informative sites are ones that are scholarly, logically organized, broad in scope, and up-to-date.

How Scholarly Is the Website?

The following questions help establish the scholarliness of a website:

- *Do the Web pages reflect authorities that are known for their expertise in the areas in which they write?*
- *Does the site emphasize primary sources when appropriate?* Primary sources are original pieces of work, such as research studies in periodicals or essays presenting an original theory.
- *How scholarly are the secondary sources?* Secondary sources are those in which someone other than the originator of the information interprets it. Stories reported in newsmagazines, such as *Time* and *Newsweek*, are usually secondary sources. Critical reviews of original research published in reputable journals tend to be high-quality secondary sources, as do book chapters that summarize research findings. The most informative secondary sources are those that refer extensively to primary sources and also critically evaluate such sources. If you are working on a research project, it is usually desirable to include reputable primary sources. By the time information has been reported by a secondary source, it is likely to have been filtered through a number of biases. The best secondary sources are those that give you enough information about the primary sources to make your own judgments.
- *Does the website evaluate its information prior to posting it?* Some sites "let anything in," while others are much more selective. Selective sites pay close attention to the authority's credentials and often provide extensive information about them.

34

- *Is the information at the site presented at a sufficiently high level of complexity, or has important information been lost for the sake of simplicity?* One way to determine the complexity of information is to ask whether it is intended for the general public or for a more select or informed audience. You should seek information that is presented at a level of complexity suitable for your purpose.

How Well Organized Is the Website?

Web page information can be best understood if it fits into a coherent overall structure. Thus, you should ask the following questions about the organization of a site:

- Is the organizational logic clear?
- Is it easy to determine its contents and links and how they are related?
- Does the design of the site allow easy and understandable navigation?
- Is it clear what is an advertisement and what is not and how the advertisements are related to the site?

How Comprehensive Is the Website?

The highest-quality websites tend to be most thorough. So you want to ask of a site:

- What is its scope?
- Does it have a large number of relevant links?
- Does it omit important information?
- Does it present multiple perspectives on an issue?

How Current Is the Information?

An advantage of the Web is that it can make new information available very quickly. Because of the rapid reproduction of information, most Web sources need to update information frequently. Thus, you need to ask these questions about a site:

- Are its references or bibliographies "cutting edge"?
- What process does the source use to update its information?
- What is the most recent update?

Look for clues to evaluate the quality of a site's content. You can obtain evaluative information from Web-based subject directories, organizations' membership directories, and magazine articles rating websites. One excellent source, which first appeared in the journal *College and Research Libraries News* in February 1994, is a column called "Internet Reviews." It provides evaluative information concerning website content. In addition, an ongoing series of articles ("Internet Resources") in the same publication lists Internet sites that provide information on subjects such as law, health and medicine, and economics. Columns similar to "Internet Reviews" can be found in *Library Journal*.

Past Performance

Like the brand names of cars, clothing, or appliances, websites develop reputations based on their perceived performance. If a website provides high-quality information, the word gets around. You should be alert to clues about a site's past performance. For example, do you encounter frequent references to the site? Have claims posted on the site held up over time, or have other sites frequently corrected them? Has the site gained a reputation for reporting false rumors? Do your instructors think highly of the site because of their prior experience with it? Ask people whom you respect about their favorite sites. Be sure to ask them why they like the site. If they give you good reasons, you can bookmark such sites.

Responding to Information from Unknown Sources

Sometimes the information available at a website is so limited that you can't determine its source. In other cases, you know who wrote it, but that is all you know.

What should you do? First, look for helpful links. For example, is there a link to a homepage that might provide a clue to the author's name, qualifications, or purpose for writing the piece? Does the URL provide a clue about the origin of the page? If you can't get further information, look for other sites. Eliminating sites whose source is unknown should speed up your search for high-quality information. There are likely to be many relevant sites whose sources you can determine. Spend your time with the sites that are most likely to provide high-quality information.

In general, you want to locate sites with the following characteristics:

- There is information about the purpose or motivation of the site.
- The page clearly indicates who is responsible for the information. There should be a link indicating who is responsible for the site.
- Multiple contact points are listed that can be used to verify the site's legitimacy.
- Sponsors or advertisers are clearly indicated.
- Other links are provided to help users learn more about what is included at the site.

Chapter 7

How Dependable Is the Authority who Provided This Information?

Suppose that, while surfing the World Wide Web, you come across the following statement concerning stare decisis:

> Law is essentially the application of prior findings to current situations. Using a well-developed common law that has been continuously developed since the 1600s, almost any situation can be related by analogy to something that has happened before. Judges look at the present cases before them and apply past precedents in a mechanistic way to current rulings. Thus, a good lawyer is one that relates his cases to as many past situations as possible, ruling out other interpretations and making the well-supported claim that the law has already been written on the subject – in his favor.

After searching a few more sites, you might come up with one that says the following:

> While judges often try to stay within the bounds of past precedent, they are people, too. They reason in a world full of context, and are thus susceptible to appeals to ethics, current political trends, and other very non-legalistic sentiments. Thus, a good lawyer supports her briefs with the law – for past precedents are important – but does not neglect the power of ethical and political arguments in her cases.

How can we decide which one to believe? Although it may seem safe to find the answer in legal studies journals, even people whom we would expect to have much expertise, such as law professors, disagree about such issues. Where do we go from here? You guessed it! Search for more information.

If you were trying to obtain additional information about whether opposites attract, one strategy is to ask, "What do other experts have to say about this?" However, experts disagree. Moreover, like the rest of us, experts are often biased and their biases may influence their conclusions.

Because experts disagree and are fallible, we need to apply our critical-thinking filters to their opinions. If we ask the right questions, we will find that some authorities possess much more expertise than others and therefore that some opinions should be more trusted than others. Consequently, one of the most important questions to ask about a Web page is "How dependable is the author of the page?" or "How much should I trust what the author has to say?"

A Special Case

The books, journals, and other resources in your college library have been evaluated to some degree—usually by a librarian or some other procedure set up by the library. Indexes and databases have usually been evaluated according to an established set of procedures or rules. In addition, articles in many journals and periodicals have been refereed (evaluated by experts) before being published. You therefore have good reason to trust information in these sources.

When you use the Web, no such evaluation has taken place. There are no governing bodies or evaluative standards. The Web is much like a magazine section in a local grocery store whose owner allows anyone in town to print a magazine and place it on rack. This analogy should help you see clearly that the ease of publishing documents on the Web results in the availability of information from authors with widely varying levels of expertise. The most reliable authorities are just a click away from the most dubious ones. The burden is on you, the user, to evaluate such authorities.

Criteria for Choosing Among Authorities

When we appeal to authorities for information, we are appealing to sources—experts—that are supposed to know more than most of us about a given topic. We believe that experts have access to certain facts and have special qualifications for drawing conclusions from those facts. You will encounter many kinds of "authorities" on the Web. Here are a few examples:

> Movie reviewers: "One of the ten best movies of the year." Valerie Viewer, *Toledo Gazette*
> Organizations: "The American Medical Association supports this position."
> Researchers: "Studies show..."

How do you choose which authorities to trust? When you look for information, you need to know the basis of the author's authority. Following are a number of questions you can ask to answer the question, "How dependable is the authority?"

Is the Authority Well-Known and Well-Regarded?
Have you encountered the name frequently in your readings or studies? Has your professor referred to the name in a positive fashion?

What Are the Authority's Credentials?
What is the author's position, institutional affiliation, and address? What organizations does she belong to? What has she done to demonstrate extensive

expertise in the area in which she is writing? Has the person had extensive experience related to the topic?

There are several ways to get information relevant to this question. First, you can check the Web page you are reading for biographical information and, if the information is not there, check links to other documents. You can also check the author's homepage.

If such checks don't work, you might try to contact the author directly to request further information about her work and professional background. Often, for example, you can obtain the author's e-mail address. You will not always receive a reply to an e-mail message, but when you do, it can be very helpful. What you are trying to discover is evidence that this expert has studied the topic thoroughly and carefully and has been judged by others to have achieved some expertise in this area.

Was the Authority in a Position to Have Especially Good Access to Pertinent Facts?

Was the author a firsthand observer of the events about which she makes claims? Has a newspaper reporter actually witnessed an event, or has she merely relied on reports from others? If the authority is not a firsthand observer, whose claims is she repeating? Why should we rely on those claims? In general, you should be more impressed by primary sources than by secondary sources.

Has the Authority Been Screened by Some Organization?

You can ask a number of questions to discern whether the author's essay has gone through some kind of screening or refereeing process to verify that it meets the standards or aims of some external evaluating body.

1. *Is the name of any organization given on the document?* Are there clues on the headers or footers that show that the document is part of a reputable academic or scholarly website? If not, are there links to other sites that provide such information?

2. *Is the organization well recognized in the relevant field of study, and is it the appropriate one for judging the content in the document?*

What Are the Likely Biases?

Is there good reason to believe that the authority is relatively free of distorting influences? Factors that can influence how evidence is reported are personal needs, prior expectations, general beliefs, attitudes, values, theories, and ideologies. These can subconsciously or deliberately affect how evidence is presented. We can't expect any authority to be totally unbiased. We can, however, expect less bias from some authorities than from others, and we can try to determine whether bias is present by seeking information about the authority's personal interest in the topic under discussion. For example, we want to be especially wary if an authority stands to benefit financially from the actions she advocates.

Authorities do not present pure facts or totally objective arguments. The information they present has been actively selected and constructed. The popularity of the Web makes it a perfect outlet for publishing documents influenced by business, social, political, and personal interests, and as a result much of the information available on the Web reflects biased uses of data. Check for biases by asking the following questions:

1. *Is the author representing any organizations that are likely to have biased agendas?* For example, is a corporation, or a "think tank" with strong political views, sponsoring the author's point of view, rather than a university or a government agency? Does the URL reveal any clues about organizations that may be sources of bias?
2. *What kinds of positions has the author taken in the past?* Do they reveal a particular set of values or perspectives?

How Scholarly and Fair Has the Author Been?

This is one of most important questions you can ask! You can evaluate the author's scholarship or relevant knowledge in the area under discussion asking the following questions:

1. Does the author refer to or show knowledge of related sources, with appropriate citations?
2. Does the author display knowledge of theories or research methods that are usually considered relevant in the treatment of this topic?
3. If claims need empirical support, does the author provide research evidence for them?
4. If the author is treating a controversial topic, does she acknowledge this and present arguments on multiple sides of the issue, or is the presentation very one-sided?
5. If it is a research document, has the author provided sufficiently detailed information about the nature of the methodology and the actual findings of the studies?
6. Does the author evaluate the information he presents? Does the author critically evaluate his own position?
7. Does the author anticipate and answer counterarguments and possible objections?
8. Does the document include a full bibliography, and does the bibliography contain references to high-quality sources, including primary sources and recent scholarly reviews?
9. Does the document show evidence that the writer is up-to-date on the topic? Do cited sources show recent dates? Does the document show a "last updated" date?

Our Inescapable Dependence on Authorities

By now you should be sensitized to the need to avoid uncritically accepting what experts have to say. However, we all must rely on experts. When a plane crashes, violence erupts, a new epidemic occurs, or we have to decide whether we need surgery for a physical ailment, we do not have the time or resources to become an expert on these issues. We frequently need the best answers we can get as quickly as possible. Thus, we cannot avoid some dependence on authorities.

We have to make decisions that require authoritative input. Knowing that some experts are much better than others is a good starting point in making such decisions. Carefully selecting which authorities to pay most attention to is a good second step. Learning to ask the critical questions that we discuss in subsequent sections of this book should also help you decide. We encourage you to be skeptical and selective, but ultimately to be decisive.

Chapter 8

What Does the Information Mean?

Suppose you are doing a report for your political science class on hate speech on the Internet. You decide to surf the Web to see what arguments are out there about this topic. The first thing you find is the following argument:

> Underlying calls for the banning of hate sites is the degraded notion that if people read hateful material they will necessarily accept it and act on it. This imparts speech with a power that it doesn't possess: the power to control your mind. The same mysticism is expressed by the International League against Racism and Anti-Semitism when they describe Nazi memorabilia as "objects that incite racial hatred." The idea is that if I see a swastika I will somehow be driven to build a gas chamber. What motivates those who want to ban hate speech today is the deep-seated belief that you can't be trusted to draw the right conclusions about things and it would be far safer if they made up your mind for you.

While you think this argument might have problems, they are not quite apparent to you, so you decide to check out other sites only to find the following counterargument:

> One of the major issues at the World Conference Against Racism (WCR) will be the regulation of hate speech and racist propaganda on the Internet. The subject of racism on the Internet has been a growing concern within UN standard-setting procedures, as reflected in United Nations-sponsored expert seminars, resolutions by the Commission of Human Rights and activities of the Office of the High Commissioner for Human Rights. Accordingly, the official UN background paper for the WCR promises that "the World Conference will focus attention on the misuse of the new technologies, in particular the Internet."

> International Convention on the Elimination of All Forms of Racial Discrimination States Parties condemn all propaganda and all organizations which are based on ideas or theories of superiority of one race or group of persons of one colour or ethnic origin, or which attempt to justify or promote racial hatred and discrimination in any form, and undertake to adopt immediate and positive measures designed to eradicate all incitement to, or acts of, such discrimination and, to this end, with due regard to the principles embodied in the Universal Declaration of Human Rights...

After reading this second site, you begin to realize the importance of thinking more deeply about the definitions of concepts within arguments. Reading these two arguments forces you to decide which concept of "person" you choose to accept, and this decision will eventually influence whether you choose to accept or reject one of the above arguments. Unfortunately, many authors (even the Great Socrates) make arguments without defining what they mean by important concepts within their argument. This chapter is designed to help you discover important words that have not been clearly defined.

Words May Have More Than One Meaning

Think about the word "success." What does it mean to you? Does it mean getting good grades in school? Does it mean making a tremendous amount of money? Does it mean being content in your job? Because language is complex, "success" could mean any of those things. Most words or phrases have multiple meanings.

If you looked up a word in a dictionary, you would likely encounter a variety of meanings for it. For example, when "run" is used as a verb, it has about fifteen meanings. If it is used as a noun, it has about twelve meanings. As an adjective, it has at least three meanings.

Suppose that you read the phrase "censoring the Internet" on a Web page. What does the author mean? Does the "Internet" mean the World Wide Web? Could it refer to electronic mail? Moreover, what type of censorship is the author referring to? Who is doing the censoring? The author knows exactly what she means by the phrase, yet these questions demonstrate that you, the reader, do not know what the author means.

When you search for information on the Internet, you will undoubtedly encounter words and phrases that have various meanings. Consequently, you need to be aware of the potential confusion associated with words and phrases.

The Need to Discover Meaning

You should be concerned about multiple meanings because they can have a serious impact on your willingness to accept an argument. You cannot respond to information unless you understand the author's intention in using a word or phrase.

Suppose that you are writing a paper for your political class about executive privilege. You type the "executive privilege" into your search engine and it brings up multiple sites. You eventually find a site that looks promising with the following argument:

> There appears to be a fairly common misperception that freedom equals license; that being free to do something means you possess an

irrevocable license to do it. What seems to be lacking is an understanding that our "rights" also confer an irrevocable responsibility to exercise our freedoms intelligently and responsibly. In the case of the behavior that led to the Communications Decency Act's passage, that meant taking reasonable precautions to ensure that pages containing questionable content (especially sexually explicit content or other, damaging, speech) were sufficiently well marked and sufficiently well secured that minors and non-consenting adults would not easily blunder into them.

This argument concludes that we should all enjoy freedom of expression. But, what does the author mean by "freedom"? Many people hold different conceptions of freedom. For example, as the following site shows some people feel that there should be absolutely no limitations on freedom of expression:

> The Internet is a powerful and positive forum for free expression. It is the place where "any person can become a town crier with a voice that resonates farther than it could from any soapbox," as the U.S. Supreme Court recently observed. Internet users, online publishers, library and academic groups and free speech and journalistic organizations share a common interest in opposing the adoption of techniques and standards that could limit the vibrance and openness of the Internet as a communications medium. Indeed, content "filtering" techniques already have been implemented in ways inconsistent with free speech principles, impeding the ability of Internet users to publish and receive constitutionally protected expression. (http://www.ifea.net)

You have identified an important source of potential confusion. Now try to use the context of the article to determine what the author means by "free." What if you cannot rely on the context for the author's meaning? If you don't know what the author means by "free," you cannot accept the argument that "The Internet is a powerful and positive forum for free expression."

In other words, before you can agree or disagree with an argument, you must be sure that you understand the author's intent in using certain key words.

Making a List of Alternative Meanings

How do you find multiple meanings of words and phrases? Here are some tools for doing so:
- *Carefully read the information and identify the argument.* Remember, you want to identify the conclusion of the argument and reasons offered to support it.
- *Identify the key words in the conclusion and reasons.* Which words seem especially important? You aren't trying to identify words or phrases that simply have multiple meanings. Almost every word on a Web page has multiple meanings. Instead, you are looking for words

that are central to the argument. You are trying to find words that could affect your willingness to accept the argument.

- *Make a list of alternative meanings for the key words.* When you identify a key word or phrase, list different meanings, interpretations, and implications of that word or phrase.

Here is an example: Suppose that you find the following information on pornography:

Many people argue that pornography is a victimless crime, but that is just because we cannot immediately see the victim. In the end, pornography destroys the heart, mind, and soul of the individual.

The author is trying to convince us that pornography is a crime that creates victims. What words or phrases are important to the author's argument? Understanding what the author means by "pornography" and "crime" is important. "Pornography" is a very unclear word. Would the author consider a very short inexplicit sex scene in a dramatic movie to be pornographic? Does the author believe that any type of nakedness is pornographic? Alternatively, are magazines like *Playboy* considered pornography? In short, we do not know precisely what the author means by pornography. Certainly, there are various degrees of potentially pornographic materials. Depending on the degree, we might be willing to agree with the author's conclusion; however, we don't know what the author believes pornography is.

Furthermore, what does the author mean by "crime"? Generally, viewing certain types of pornography is not a crime. Thus, does the author mean that viewing pornography is a crime in the sense that the viewer is breaking a law and deserves to be punished? Alternatively, does the author mean that the viewer is committing a crime because he or she is doing something that is morally offensive? Because the author is trying to convince us that pornography is a crime, we should understand what he or she means by "crime."

Get into the habit of generating at least two possible meanings for a key word and thinking about how those meanings affect your willingness to accept the author's conclusion. Focus on key words and make a list of their potential meanings.

Use Caution When Your Meaning Differs from That of the Information-Provider

Let's return to the freedom of expression example. Because the author did not make it clear that her understanding of free expression was quite different from other conceptions of expression, you may not have been able to determine her understanding of "free." When you cannot determine the author's intended meaning you should be wary of relying on that information. Why?

Suppose that you went to several different websites for information to include in a paper about free expression on the Internet. Some of those websites used one definition of free while others used more limited understanding. If you did not identify the differences between the definitions, your paper would probably be quite confusing and maybe even incorrect.

Think about this example. You are asked to write a paper about the morality of the death penalty. Before you conduct any searches on the Internet, you should determine what you will mean by "death penalty." You might believe that death by lethal injection is morally acceptable; yet you would argue that electrocution is morally unacceptable.

Suppose that you decide that in your paper you will argue that the death penalty, in the form of lethal injection only, is morally acceptable. You conduct an Internet search to find information about the death penalty and lethal injections. At "Execution Methods Used by States" (http://www.fcc.state.fl.us/fcc/reports/methods/emstates.html#probs), you encounter the following information:

> As of June 15, 1997, twenty-two executions encountered problems
> during the execution process.

What should you do with this information? The author says that twenty-two executions encountered problems. But you don't know what kinds of executions had problems. What if *all* of these executions were by lethal injection? On the other hand, what if *none* of them was by lethal injection? You need to find out what the author means by "executions" because this information could strongly support or weaken your argument.

In summary, if you are searching for a certain definition of a word or phrase and want to rely on that information, make sure that your intended meaning matches the author's intended meaning.

Use Your Purpose as a Guide When Searching for Meaning

Now that you have learned to pay attention to multiple meanings, you have learned that you must be more careful in reading and selecting information. Your Internet search may therefore become more difficult.

For example, previously you could simply type "pornography" and start reading the enormous amounts of information retrieved by the search engine. Now you must pay close attention to the potential meaning of "pornography" on each site. On the other hand, careful attention to meanings might also save you time in conducting more narrow searches for information. For example, instead of simply typing "death penalty," you could type "lethal injection."

Your purpose in searching for certain information can serve as a guide for determining meaning. For example, if you are writing a paper about the death penalty, you should determine what you mean by "death penalty" before you write the paper. In contrast, if you are attempting to arrive at an opinion about abortion, you might not want to limit your definition just yet. Instead, you might want to read numerous Web pages to see how, or if, they define "abortion" and "human life." Thus, your purpose can guide you as you search for the meanings of certain words and phrases.

In conclusion, use the purpose of your search as a guide when searching for the meanings of unclear words and phrases. Sometimes it will help to narrowly define a key word before you search; however, be aware that a narrow definition might not be appropriate in some situations.

Chapter 9

What Are the Value Assumptions?

Suppose you are asked to write an environmental policy paper. You are to explore whether industrial pollution is better controlled through deregulation and tax incentives than through regulation, punitive fees, and disclosure. You hop on the Web to look for some information, arguments, and statistics. The first place you stop has the following argument:

> Taxes and tax incentives can be used in many ways to promote new and cleaner ways of doing business. Tax incentives have been used successfully to help new technologies such as solar energy and wind power to achieve economies of scale and experience, reducing their production costs and moving them toward commercial viability. Tax programs can stimulate institutional changes that permanently transform the market, such as the creation of recycling collection networks. Several states have devised tax tools to encourage pollution prevention. (http://www.sustainableeconomy.org/taxcode.htm)

After looking over this site for a few minutes, you decide to look for other perspectives. You find a site that argues the following:

> From a policy-making perspective, our analysis thus offers two important results. First, the presence of clear and strong standards accompanied with a significant and credible penalty system does send appropriate signals to the regulated community which then responds with a lowering of pollution emissions. Secondly, the public disclosure of environmental performance does create additional and strong incentives for pollution control. These results do suggest that both regulation and information belongs to the regulator's arsenal.
> (http://www.worldbank.org/nipr/work_paper/andor/andora05.htm#P1935_151105)

Clearly, these two authors disagree. How do you decide which author is correct? It seems that both authors are interpreting the facts of the issue quite differently. Why might this be? It seems that they both value different things in this world and that these different values might have influenced their arguments. In this chapter, we will talk more about values and the ways in which they influence the arguments of those on the Internet.

After studying Chapter 2, you know how to identify reasons and conclusions in an argument. You know that a conclusion is only as good as the reasons given to support it. But there is more to the structure of an argument than reasons and conclusions. Consider this example:

Convicted felons should not be allowed to hold public office.

Here is the basic structure of this argument:

Conclusion: Convicted felons cannot be trusted to make policy decisions.
Reason: Convicted felons have no respect for the law.

Does this argument make sense? Does the conclusion follow from the reason? At first glance the argument seems sound. The reason is correct: A convicted (and confessed) criminal has displayed contempt for the law. But does it follow that they can never be trusted? Hidden within the argument are certain assumptions that we must accept to accept the argument. The author is assuming that individuals are either completely honest or completely dishonest. Consequently, a person who has broken the law once will break the law at every opportunity. This argument makes no sense as its flip side is that a basically honest person will never break the law. The reason in this argument is true, but without the assumption, the conclusion does not follow from the reasoning.

An argument consists of reasons plus a conclusion, but assumptions must be added into the structure. The argument now looks something like this:

Reason: Convicted felons have proven themselves untrustworthy.
Assumption: Policymakers must be trustworthy.
Conclusion: Convicted felons should not be allowed to hold public office.

These assumptions are critical to understanding the argument, but unfortunately, most authors do not reveal them. It is *your* job to hunt for them. This chapter will help you discover assumptions by giving you tips on what to look for and where to look.

Discovering Values

Before attempting to identify value *assumptions*, you need to have a clear understanding of what a value is. For the purposes of this book, we will define the word "value" as an idea that people see as worthwhile. In the example above you we saw that the author of the passage held the value of trustworthiness. She saw public trust as an idea that was worthwhile.

Let's try to make a list of common values. (Remember that values are ideas that people find worthwhile. A favorite CD may be very important to you, but it is not an idea that will affect your conclusions.) It may help if you focus on ideas that are so important to you that they affect many of the decisions you make. These ideas will most likely be your values.

A second definition of values should be helpful. Think of values as standards of behavior that we endorse and expect people to meet. How do you expect the people around you to behave? Most likely, these expectations are rooted in your values.

Also, make sure your list contains only those values that most affect your behavior. Certain values have more consequences than others, and the ones that will most likely affect arguments are the only ones we need to identify in evaluating Internet sites. For example, the author of a pro-life website may value politeness, but that value will make little or no difference in her argument.

We list some commonly-held values below; perhaps that will help you think of other values for your list. When you look over the list, think about which values stand out as most and as least important in your life.

Common Values

adventure
altruism
ambition
autonomy
collective responsibility
comfort
competitions
cooperation
courage
creativity
efficiency
equality of condition
equality of opportunity
excellence
flexibility

freedom of speech
generosity
harmony
honesty
justice
novelty
order
patriotism
peace
rationality
security
spontaneity
tolerance
tradition
wisdom

Discovering Value Assumptions

Look at the Origin of the Website

An important clue to discovering value assumptions is the background of the authors. Almost anyone can create a website, and all authors have different agendas. The value assumptions of the author may be obvious if you know the author's background. For example, if you go to http://www.aclu.org, you will have linked to a Web page sponsored by the American Civil Liberties Union. Obviously, this is a group that tries to protect the civil liberties of Americans. This objective implies that its members value freedom over order. This value assumption is implicit within many of its arguments. You may find an argument similar to this on their website:

Freedom of speech is crucial on college campuses. Education is about sharing opinions and ideas. Even if the ideas are harmful or offensive, they should not be restricted.

The value assumption of freedom over order is crucial to the validity of this argument. If people value order over freedom, they will not agree that all freedom of expression is important on a college campus. Sometimes freedom of expression leads to violent acts, and those who value order and security more than freedom of speech would feel that freedom of expression is not, in this instance, important on college campuses.

If we know where a website originated, it is easier to evaluate the argument because we have better ideas about the author's value assumptions.

Think About What Is Important to Those Who Disagree

Another useful way to identify value conflicts is to ask yourself, "What would those who disagree with this website care about?" Let's try an example. While searching the Web, you find this argument about same-sex marriages:

Same gender couples should be given the same opportunity to share in the rights, responsibilities, and commitments of a civil marriage because marriage is a basic human right.

Now, ask yourself what those who disagree with this conclusion would be most concerned about. In many cases, those who disagree feel that allowing same-sex marriage will be violating the tradition of marriage in society. To them this concern is more important than equality. In other words, those who disagree value tradition more than they value equality in this situation. Therefore, the value conflict in this issue is between equality and tradition, and the author of the website makes the value assumption that equality should be preferred over tradition.

In summary, assumptions are hidden ideas that are influential yet are taken for granted. Value assumptions occur when an author implicitly assumes that one value should be preferred over other values in certain contexts. Looking at the author's background and the values of those who disagree will provide clues to an author's value assumptions.

Chapter 10

How Good
Is the Evidence?

Suppose you are to write a paper on advocacy groups and public policy for your political science class. After surfing the Web a bit, you come upon the following information:

> The effect of interest groups on public policy is very real but generally limited. Interest groups overly represent wealthy interests, which is a minority in the United States. In addition, economic interest groups would rather their activities remain unknown, unlike ideological interest groups that seek the television camera. Thus economic interest group activity operates in a limited realm, for limited goals, and with relatively limited effects. This is not to say that economic interest group activity is benign, because often times it produces waste and special advantages. This is itself unfair to the rest of us who do not enjoy similar advantages and who must subsidize those advantages, and hurtful to democracy when it appears the principle of equal representation has been violated.
> (http://www.dacc.edu/~chantz/Interestgroups.htm)

After taking notes at this site, you move on to the next site, which presents you with this contrasting information:

> With campaign finance reform being widely debated and understood, even the most understated and cautious of politicians admit that Congress is sold out to special interest groups, that the political system runs on campaign contributions (legalized bribes), and that governmental decisions are made in response to them. However you want to describe political realities, the bottom-line reality is that government is corrupt, in the hands of big money contributors, special interests, and the rich and powerful.
> (http://www.pnpa.com/distribution/denenberg/column99.htm)

Given that both of these websites disagree, how would you decide which site's information to use? It seems that you're going to have to have some tool to evaluate the extent to which the evidence for one site is better than the other. In this chapter, we will be giving you the tools to evaluate such evidence.

What Is the Relationship Between "Facts" and Evidence?

Most websites present beliefs that the communicator wants us to accept as "facts." These beliefs can be opinions, conclusions, reasons, or assumptions. Let's refer to such beliefs as *factual claims*.

The first question you should ask about any factual claim is, *"Why should I believe it?"* The next question is, *"Does the claim need evidence to support it?"* Is there any reason to doubt the claim? If so, there is a need for supporting evidence. If there is no evidence, the claim is an *unsupported opinion*. You should seriously question opinions that need to be backed up by evidence but are not.

The quality of evidence varies greatly. If there is evidence, your next question is, *"How good is the evidence?"* Some factual claims can be counted on more than others. For example, you probably feel quite certain that the claim "Most CEOs in the biggest 100 corporations are men" is true, but less certain that the assertion "Parental co-sleeping with infants helps make them more secure as an adult."

We want to ask of factual claims, "Can we count on such beliefs?"—at least for the time being. The greater the quality and quantity of evidence supporting a claim, the more we can depend on it and call it a "fact." The major difference between claims that are opinions and those that are facts lies in the evidence. The more supporting evidence there is for a belief, the more "factual" the belief becomes.

Before we judge the persuasiveness of a Web communication, we need to know which factual claims are most dependable. To determine dependability, we ask questions like the following:

*   What is your proof?
*   Where's the evidence?
*   How do you know that's true?
*   Why do you believe that?

Internet sites that provide good evidence for their factual claims show respect for users of their site. They communicate that they expect us to accept their claims only if they have made a convincing case for them through the use of good evidence. Sites that fail to present needed evidence treat the user as an unthinking fool rather than as a critical thinker. You should avoid such sites.

Kinds of Evidence

To evaluate evidence, we first need to ask, "What kind of evidence is it?" This tells us what further questions to ask. The most frequently used kinds of evidence are:

53

- Appeals to authorities
- Personal testimonials
- Personal experience
- Case studies
- Research studies

Let us take a closer look at each of these. We have already addressed this topic in previous chapters. Here we just want to remind you of the frequency of this type of evidence.

Personal Testimonials and Personal Experience as Evidence

"I home-schooled my child, and now she's doing great in college."
"In only six weeks, I lost ten pounds, using Lesflab. I highly recommend it to you."
"I really enjoyed his class. You should take it."

A common strategy to support a claim is to present direct "testimonials" or "endorsements" from individuals who have had experiences related to it. Such claims are widely used in promoting books, movies, politicians, diets, medical practices, and positions on social issues such as gun control and abortion.

In most cases we should pay little attention to personal testimonials until we find out much more about the expertise, interests, values, and biases behind them. We should be especially sensitive to the following problems with testimonials:

1   *Selectivity.* People's experiences differ greatly. Those who are trying to persuade us have usually carefully selected the testimony they use. We should always ask, What was the experience like for those whom we have not heard from?

2.   *Personal interest.* Many testimonials come from people who have something to gain from their testimony. For example, authors will sometimes provide positive testimonials for others, expecting that the favor will be returned when their book is reviewed. Always ask, Does the person providing the testimony have a relationship with what he or she is advocating such that we can expect a strong bias in his or her testimony?

3.   *Omitted information.* Testimonials rarely provide sufficient information about the basis for the judgment. For example, when a friend of yours raves about a certain teacher, you should ask *why*. Our standards may differ from those of the person giving the testimony.

In general, be cautious about using either your own personal experiences or those of just a few others as evidence to support a belief. Because people differ so much, personal experiences lead us to over generalize. Single experiences can demonstrate that certain outcomes are possible; for example, you may have met someone who smoked three packs of cigarettes a day and lived to the age of 90.

54

Such experiences by themselves, however, can't prove that such outcomes are typical.

Research Studies as Evidence

Studies show...
Researchers have found...
A recent report in the *New England Journal of Medicine* indicates...

One form of evidence that often carries special weight is the research study: a systematic collection of observations by people trained to do scientific research. How dependable are research findings? We can't tell until we ask questions.

Because the scientific method attempts to avoid many biases in our observations and in our intuition and common sense, it has a number of advantages over other methods. Above all, it seeks *publicly verifiable data*—that is, data collected under conditions such that other qualified people can make similar observations and check the results. A second major characteristic is *control*: It minimizes extraneous factors that might affect the accuracy and interpretation of claims.

While there is much more to science than we can discuss here, we want you to remember that scientific research, when conducted well, is one of the best evidence sources. Such research avoids some of the disadvantages of case studies, appeals to authority, and personal testimonials. However, it has some important limitations.

Limitations of Scientific Research
Most questions, particularly those that focus on complex human behavior, can be answered only tentatively even with the best research evidence. When communicators appeal to research as a source of evidence, you should consider these factors:

Research Varies Greatly in Quality
We should rely more on some research studies than on others. Because the research process is so complex and subject to so many external influences, even well-trained researchers sometimes conduct flawed studies; publication in a scientific journal does not guarantee that a research study is not flawed in important ways.

Research Findings Often Contradict One Another
Single research studies presented outside the context of the set of studies of the question at hand often provide misleading conclusions. Research findings that most deserve our attention are those that are presented as part of an extensive set of related findings.

Research Findings Do Not Prove Conclusions

At best, findings *support* conclusions. Researchers must always interpret their findings, and all findings can be interpreted in more than one way. Thus, researchers' conclusions should not be treated as demonstrated "truths."

Researchers Are Biased

Researchers have expectations, attitudes, values, and needs that can bias the questions they ask, the way they conduct their research, and the way they interpret their findings. Despite efforts to avoid bias, science is not a neutral, value-free, totally objective enterprise. Scientists often have an emotional or financial interest in a particular hypothesis. For example, researchers who are directly funded by a major drug company may be more likely to find positive treatment results for that company's drugs than researchers who have no personal relationship with the drug company. Like all fallible human beings, researchers may find it difficult to objectively treat data that conflict with their interests.

Web Authors Often Distort or Simplify Research Conclusions

Major discrepancies may occur between the conclusion merited by the original research and the use of the evidence to support a communicator's beliefs. For example, researchers may carefully qualify their own conclusions in their original research report only to have others use the conclusions without the qualifications.

Research "Facts" Change Over Time, Especially Claims About Human Behavior

Today's "truths" are frequently disconfirmed by later research.

Research Varies in How Artificial It Is

Because of the need to control the research process, research may lose some of its "real-world" quality. The more artificial the research, the more difficult it is to generalize from the research study to the world outside. The problem of artificiality is especially evident in studies of complex social behavior. For example, to study the effects of television violence, researchers may expose children to violent cartoons and then observe how aggressive they are toward dolls. We should ask, Is aggressive behavior toward dolls too artificial to tell us much about aggressive behavior in other situations?

Questions for Evaluating Research Studies

The ability to evaluate research evidence requires an in-depth understanding of research methodologies and philosophies that this book can't provide for you. We can, however, present some questions that you can ask about research evidence.

1.   What is the quality of the source of the report? Usually, the most dependable reports are those published in peer-review journals, in which a study is not accepted until it has been reviewed by a series of relevant experts. Usually—but not always—the more reputable the

56

source, the better designed the study. So try to find out all you can about the source's reputation.

2.   Other than the quality of the source, are there other clues included in the communication suggesting that the research was well done? For example, does the report detail any special strengths of the research?

3.   Have conclusions from the study been supported by other findings? For example, when an association such as the link between smoking and cancer is repeatedly and consistently found in well-designed studies, there is reason to believe it, at least until those who disagree can provide persuasive evidence for their point of view.

4.   How selective has the communicator been in choosing studies? For example, have relevant studies with contradictory results been omitted? Has the communicator selected only studies that support his or her point?

5.   Is there any evidence of critical thinking? Has the speaker or writer shown a critical attitude toward earlier research that supports his or her point of view? Most conclusions from research need to be qualified in some way. Has the communicator demonstrated a willingness to qualify her conclusions?

6.   Is there any reason for someone to have distorted the research? We need to be wary of situations in which the researchers need to find certain kinds of results.

7.   Are conditions in the research artificial and therefore distorted? Always ask: How similar are the research conditions to the situation the researcher is generalizing about?

8.   How far can we generalize, given the research sample? (We discuss this question in depth in the next section.)

9.   Are there any biases or distortions in the surveys, questionnaires, ratings, or other measurements that the researcher uses? We need to be confident that the researcher's measurements are accurate. The problem of biased surveys and questionnaires is so pervasive that we discuss it in more detail in the next section.

Biased Surveys and Questionnaires

Surveys and questionnaires are usually used to measure people's attitudes and beliefs. Responses to them are subject to many influences; one therefore must be very cautious in interpreting their meaning. Let's examine some of these influences.

First, for survey responses to be meaningful, participants must respond honestly. What people say needs to match what they truly believe and feel. Yet individuals frequently shade the truth. For example, they may give answers that they think they ought to give, or they may experience hostility toward the questionnaire or toward the kind of question being asked. They may give too little thought to the question.

Remember: You cannot assume that survey responses accurately reflect true attitudes.

Second, the wording of many survey questions is ambiguous; the questions therefore are subject to multiple interpretations. As a result, different individuals may in effect be responding to different questions! For example, imagine the possible interpretations of the following question: "Are you happily married?" The more ambiguous the wording of a question, the less credible the results. You should always ask: How were the questions worded?

Third, questionnaires may contain many kinds of built-in biases, including biased wording and biased context. A small change in how a question is worded can have a major effect on how it is answered. Here is an example:

A U.S. congressman sent a questionnaire to his constituents and received the following results: 92 percent were against government-supported child-care centers.

Let's look closely at the survey question: "Do you believe the federal government should provide child-care centers to assist parents in rearing their children?" Do you see the bias built into the question? The "leading" words are "to assist parents in rearing their children." The responses would have been quite different if the question had read: "Do you believe the federal government should provide child-care centers to assist parents who are unable to find alternative child care while they are working?" Thus, the responses obtained by the congressman do not accurately reflect attitudes concerning child-care centers.

Other factors that influence questionnaire responses are the placement of the items relative to other items, the questionnaire's length, and the need to please or displease the researcher or other groups that might use the survey for their own purposes.

Some surveys are better done than others. The better its quality, the more you should be influenced by survey results. Examine survey procedures carefully before accepting survey results. Once you have ascertained the quality of the procedures, you can generate your own qualified generalization—one that takes into account any biases you might have found.

For example, if the respondents in a survey are subscribers to a "liberal" magazine, you should apply any resulting generalization only to people who subscribe to that magazine. Even biased surveys can be informative; but you need to know the biases in order not to be unduly persuaded by the findings.

In summary, our focus in this chapter has been the evaluation of evidence. We have discussed four kinds of evidence: *appeals to authority, testimonials, case studies,* and *research studies.* Each kind has its strengths and weaknesses. Usually you can rely most on claims that authors support directly with extensive scientific research. However, many issues have not been settled by scientific research, and communicators therefore must rely on inconclusive research and on other kinds of evidence. You should be especially wary of claims supported by inappropriate authorities, personal testimonials, vivid case studies, or poorly designed research studies. When you encounter *any* evidence, you should try to determine its quality by asking, "How good is the evidence?"

Chapter 11

What Significant Information Is Omitted?

At http://sun.soci.niu.edu/~critcrim/guns/gun.viol, we find this information:

> Approximately 60 percent of all murder victims in the United States in 1989 (about 12,000 people) were killed with firearms. According to estimates, firearm attacks injured another 70,000 victims, some of whom were left permanently disabled. In 1985 (the latest year for which data are available), the cost of shootings—either by others, through self-inflicted wounds, or in accidents—was estimated to be more than $14 billion nationwide for medical care, long-term disability, and premature death. Among firearms, handguns are the murder weapon of choice. While handguns make up only about one-third of all firearms owned in the United States, they account for 80 percent of all murders committed with firearms.

On the other hand, the author of another website claims:

> There are numerous protective uses of guns. A recent study concluded that there are between 700,000 and 2 million protective uses of guns each year. Another study argued that there are as many as 75 lives protected by a gun for every life lost to a gun.

Are you looking for statistics to help you decide what position to take in arguments about gun control? You could find lots of them. However, the two passages just quoted indicate that you need to worry about an important problem when you use Web information in making decisions about such controversial issues. The information that you find at any particular site is selective. Other important information is almost always omitted.

The Importance of Looking for Omitted Information

How compelling are the following advertisements?

> Most doctors prescribe Ease-Pain for headaches!
> Jump-Start Cola was Number 1 in recent taste tests!

The purpose of both advertisements is, of course, to persuade you to buy more of the designated product. In such advertisements, as well as in more complex arguments, what is *not said* is often more informative than what is *said*. For example, if the Ease-Pain company gives bigger discounts to hospitals than other aspirin manufacturers do, gives hospitals more free samples, or offers cruises to physicians who use its product, this information is unlikely to be included in the ad—even though it may be highly relevant to judging the merit of the advertising claim.

By asking the questions you have learned in earlier chapters, such as those concerning the credibility of authorities and the quality of evidence, you will detect much missing information. However, your search needs to be more complete. This is an important additional question that you must ask in order to judge the quality of reasoning: What significant information is omitted? By "significant omitted information" we mean information that would affect whether you should be influenced by an author's arguments.

When you have finished this chapter, you should be familiar with three good ways to decide whether a website has presented a good argument. The best arguments are ones that are supported by reasons that

- Are relevant to the truth of the conclusion
- Are acceptable or well supported
- Have not omitted important information

The Inevitability of Incomplete Information

Incomplete reasoning is inevitable for several reasons. First, there are the limitations imposed by time and space. Arguments are incomplete because communicators do not have an infinite amount of time in which to organize them; and usually they do not have unlimited space or time in which to present them. Second, most of us have a limited attention span; we get bored when messages are too long. Communicators therefore often feel a need to get their message across quickly. Advertisements and editorials reflect both these factors.

Third, the communicator's knowledge is always incomplete. For example, when half the doctors sampled in a survey of attitudes toward managed care fail to complete the questionnaire, the researcher can't know whether they differ in significant ways from doctors who do complete the survey. Yet this is a very important piece of information in judging the survey's dependability.

A fourth reason information is omitted is outright attempts to deceive. Advertisers know that they are omitting key bits of information. If they were to describe all the chemicals or component parts that go into their products, you would be less likely to buy them. Experts in every field consciously omit information when open disclosure would weaken the persuasive effect of their advice. Their goal is to persuade you, not to fully inform you.

A fifth important reason is differences in values, beliefs, and attitudes. When communicators approach an issue from one perspective, they may not be aware of other perspectives. A particular perspective is like a pair of blinders on a horse. The blinders cause the horse to focus on what is directly in front of it. Similarly, an individual's perspective may prevent him or her from noting information presented by those with differing perspectives.

Questions for Identifying Omitted Information

Because of the importance of detecting missing information, you need to remind yourself again and again to actively search for omitted information. How do you search, and what do you expect to find?

Many kinds of questions can help you identify relevant omitted information. Some of the questions you have already learned to ask will highlight important omitted information. In addition, you should always ask yourself, "Has the Web page left out any other information that I need to know before I judge the quality of its reasoning?"

Here are common kinds of significant omitted information and questions you can ask to help fill in what is missing:

- **Common counterarguments**
  What reasons would someone who disagrees offer?
  Are there research studies that contradict the studies presented?
  Are there missing examples, testimonials, or analogies that support the other side of the argument?

- **Missing definitions**
  How would the arguments differ if key terms were defined in other ways?

- **Missing value preferences or perspectives**
  From what other set of values might one approach this issue?
  What kinds of arguments would someone approaching the issue from a different set of values make?

- **Origins of "facts" alluded to in the argument**
  Where do the "facts" come from?
  Are the factual claims supported by well-done research or by reliable sources?

- **Details of procedures used for gathering facts**
  How many people completed the questionnaire? Were they randomly selected?
  How were the survey questions worded?
  Were the participants aware of the researcher's hypothesis?

- **Alternative techniques for gathering or organizing the evidence**
  How might the results from an interview study differ from written questionnaire results?

- **Missing or incomplete figures, graphs, tables, or data**
  Would the figure look different if it included evidence from earlier or later years?
  Has the author "stretched" the figure to make the differences look larger?

- **Omitted effects, both positive and negative, and both short- and long-term, of what is advocated and is opposed**
  Has the argument left out important positive or negative consequences of a proposed action?
  Do we need to know the impact of the action in any of the following areas: political, social, economic, biological, spiritual, health, interpersonal, or environmental?

- **Context of quotes and testimonials**
  Has a quote or testimonial been taken out of context?

- **Benefits accruing to the author from convincing others to follow her advice**
  Will the author benefit financially if we adopt her proposed policy?

Let's examine an argument that has omitted some of the types of information just listed and observe how each omission might cause us to form a faulty conclusion.

> Violent crime is rising in U.S. schools, according to a government survey of 10,000 students ages 12 to 19. The study, conducted by the Education and Justice departments, shows that while the overall crime rate at U.S. schools is relatively stable, violent crime is on the rise. Comparing data from 1989 and 1995, the researchers found:
>
> > 15 percent of students say they are crime victims and 4 percent say the offenses involved violence.
> > 65 percent say they can buy drugs at school.
> > 28 percent report gangs at school, an increase of almost 100 percent.
> > 13 percent say they know students who bring guns to school along with their books.
>
> It is time to pass the president's plan and spend more money on juvenile crime; we need many more prosecutors and after-school programs.

What important information do you need to know before you can decide whether to support the president's plan?

To begin, what are possible meanings of the phrase "violent crime is on the rise"? It is not clear, for example, what is meant by "violent crime". Also, what do students mean when they say they are crime victims, and what does the phrase "involved violence" mean? "Crime victim" and "involved violence" can mean very different things to different students, and the more serious the crimes they are referring to the more concerned we are likely to be.

Are there missing or incomplete figures, graphs, tables, or data? For example, would the figures look different if they included evidence from the years between 1989 and 1995? We do not have sufficient data to determine a consistent trend. Perhaps 1995 was an atypical year. Also, what was the rate of violent crime before 1989? We could also ask whether the decreases have been greater for some groups or school settings than others, and whether that has implications for our feelings of safety. In addition, the report does not tell us how many gangs were actually *operating* in schools, only how many students were *aware* of gangs. It's possible that gangs have become more visible, which would increase student awareness.

How about the origins of the "facts" alluded to? Has the data been collected in a trustworthy fashion? Were any biases operating to influence these numbers? All of the numbers are based on self-reports of students, rather than on unbiased observations of others. Is it possible that students were more willing to report violent acts in 1995 than in 1989 because they had been sensitized to violence in the media? Also, maybe students were more willing to report the presence of gangs in 1995 than in previous years.

Are there specific value preferences or perspectives that influence the reasoning? For example, does the emphasis on government intervention as the solution keep certain other possibilities hidden, such as developing local programs that encourage greater family responsibility, or encouraging an educational campaign for children? Also, what are possible negative long-term effects of the president's plan?

Would other research methods give us a different view of the crime situation? Do we need something more than numbers of crimes? For example, would interviews with, or surveys of, people living in traditionally high-crime areas gives us a different picture of whether we're winning the war against crime? Are there events we are not measuring that we should be measuring, such as changes in the rates of parents providing after-school supervision, or changes in the numbers of children at high-risk ages? Will more kids and less control equal more crime?

As you can see, there may be an important hidden side to the findings. We have only a partial picture. Unless we complete the picture, our decisions about whether to support present crime fighting policies, or whether to feel safe in our communities, will be uninformed.

The Importance of Possible Long-Term Negative Consequences

The following argument recently appeared on several Internet sites:

> The government should require that all infants and toddlers be restrained on airplanes as they are in cars. The National Transportation Safety Board says that since 1989, at least three unrestrained children under 2 have died in plane crashes in which some passengers survived and has recommended child restraints in planes since 1990.

The goal of requiring child restraints is to make flying safer for infants. But what if such a requirement has unintended consequences? For example, what if such a requirement adds so much to the cost of flying that fewer parents fly and travel by car instead, and in the long run more infants are killed in car accidents than would have been killed in plane crashes?

One type of omitted information is especially important yet it is often overlooked: potential negative effects. Proposals for action are usually presented in terms of their benefits, such as greater safety, increased choice and speed, better appearance, more leisure, increased length of life, or more and/or improved commodities. However, because most actions have both positive and negative impacts, we need to ask several questions:

- Might the action have unintended consequences?
- Which segments of society do *not* benefit from a proposed action? Who loses? What do the losers have to say about it?
- How does the proposed action affect the distribution of power? Which groups gain and which groups lose?
- How does a particular action affect how we view the world: what we think, how we think, and what we know and can know?
- What effects might the action have on our health? Are there significant side effects, for example?
- How does the action affect how we relate to other people and to the environment?

For each of these questions, we also want to ask, "What are the potential long-term negative effects of the action?"

Once you know what information is missing, you have a much better sense of the quality of reasoning and what you don't know that you need to know. You must now decide whether it is possible to arrive at a conclusion without the missing information.

We have pointed out that reasoning is always incomplete. Thus, to claim that you can't make a decision as long as information is missing would prevent you from ever forming any opinions. All the information you need to be absolutely certain that you are right will never be available. You need to do the best you can with the information you can obtain.

Chapter 12

Are There Rival Causes?

Suppose you have been assigned a paper for your political science class on the subject of the causes of "voter apathy." While this may seem like a simple question, it turns out that it is much more complicated than you thought. At the first site you visited, you found the following argument:

> Martin Wattenberg, a nationally known UCI political scientist who studies the causes of voter apathy. He believes one of many contributing factors is the proliferation of TV channels and Internet sites, which make it easier than ever for people to avoid public-affairs news entirely. The changing media environment, he says, has had a particular impact on today's young citizens, who have never known a time when national political events received blanket coverage on all TV channels. Wattenberg has a simple suggestion for helping increase turnout: Declare Election Day a national holiday to give people more time to get to the polls. (http:// www.today.uci.edu/tips/00tips/0002.html)

Yet, the next website you go to thinks voter apathy is caused by something else:

> Since Watergate, we have witnessed an increased cynicism about our governmental institutions. We see its impact in declining voter participation and apathy about our public life--symptoms of a system that demands reform. But it's a mistake, I think, to believe that this apathy means Americans do not love their country and aren't motivated to fix what is wrong. The growth of local volunteerism and the outpouring of sentiment for "the greatest generation" suggest a different explanation: that Americans hunger for patriotic service to the nation, but do not see ways to personally make a difference.

As you can see, whenever you ask a causal question, you are bound to get multiple answers. Almost all facts about the world have multiple explanations. In this chapter you will learn how to spot rival causes within arguments.

The Need to Search for Other Possible Causes

The issue of what causes teen drinking illustrates a frequent question that we might ask from a search of websites: "What causes something to happen?" For example, we might search the Web for information to help us answer questions like the following:

What caused the murder rate to decrease in the United States in 1999?

Why has the rate of depression among teenagers increased over the last 10 years?

Does walking three times a week reduce the likelihood of heart disease?

A common difficulty in using evidence to prove that something caused something else is the possibility of *rival causes*. The above interpretations of the causes of voter apathy show that the same evidence can be consistent with different interpretations. When those interpretations focus on the causes of events, we refer to them as rival causes.

Both experts and non-experts frequently emphasize one cause to explain events or research findings when other causes could also explain them. Usually, these experts will not reveal rival causes to you; you will have to identify them. Doing so can be especially helpful as you decide "how good is the evidence?" because the more plausible rival causes you can think of, the less confidence you should have in the cause proposed by the writer. Whenever you notice an author making a claim about the cause of something, always ask: Are there rival causes?

Knowing When to Look for Rival Causes

When should you look for rival causes? Whenever you notice causal thinking. As commonly used the term "cause" means "to bring about, make happen, influence, or affect." Communicators indicate causal thinking in many ways.

Following are some claims from recent articles that use language indicating the presence of causal reasoning:

* Why do college students drink so stupidly? Because drinking intelligently is against the law.
* Animal therapy reduces anxiety.
* Visitors boost their risk of heart attacks by 34 percent during their stay in New York.
* Smoking during pregnancy fosters violent crime.
* Marriage brings considerable benefits to both women and men.
* Writing about trauma eases illness.
* Religious attendance improves health.

The Pervasiveness of Rival Causes

On April 20, 1999, 13 people were killed and more than two dozen were wounded when two young men dressed in black overcoats and masks opened fire inside Columbine High School in Littleton, Colorado. The gunmen were seniors at the school and members of a student clique called the "Trenchcoat Mafia." The shootings captured the nation's attention, and Internet sites suggested many possible causes for the violent behavior.

One site dismisses many possible previously suggested causes, such as violent movies and the Internet, and instead blames "our experiences in life," citing several pieces of evidence in support of this cause, such as the fact that many Columbine athletes had treated the two teenagers badly and that the two were often called names, such as "dirtbag" and "faggot."

The results of a Gallup poll are discussed at another site. In response to the poll, all of the following causes were suggested by teenagers: problems of peer relations and peer pressures, personal problems of the killers—they were sick, angry, confused, etc., ignoring of warning signals, and parental factors. In contrast, the poll found that adults mainly blamed parents and families. Other causes mentioned by adults were personal problems of the gunmen, lack of morals and religion in society, and the prevalence of violence in the media.

A third site suggests that the cause might be the current legal framework, which encourages moral mediocrity and facilitates the culture of violence that is influencing today's youth.

Now, let's leave Columbine and examine something very different in need of a causal explanation—the findings of a research study. The report is similar in form to many such reports on the Web:

> A researcher reported that treating headaches with relaxation exercises and biofeedback is helpful. Three-fourths of 95 people with chronic tension headaches and about half of 75 migraine suffers studied reduced the frequency and severity of their headaches after learning how to relax head, neck, and shoulder muscles and control stress and tension with biofeedback.

In this study, the researcher probably began with the hypothesis that relaxation training causes reduction of headache suffering, and he found evidence consistent with that hypothesis. But consider some rival, or alternative, causes for the same findings:

1. Research participants were highly suggestible, and the expectation of improvement was responsible for the change; like the sugar pill placebo effect in medicine, thinking they were going to get better might have stimulated a number of physical and mental processes that caused them to feel better.

2. Participants wanted to please the researchers; they therefore reported feeling better even though they did not.

3. Most participants volunteered while undergoing highly stressful situations; they experienced a reduction in stress during the course of the study, and this reduction accounted for the reduction in symptoms.

Some important lessons can be learned from the Columbine shootings and the research study.

Lessons Learned

- Many kinds of events may have rival causes. They include clinical case studies, criminal trials, research studies, advertising statistics, sports page charts, airline crash findings, and historical events.
- Experts can examine the same evidence and identify different causes to explain it.
- Although many explanations can fit the facts, some seem more plausible than others.
- Most communicators will provide only the causes they favor. The critical thinker must generate rival causes.
- Generating rival causes is a creative process; usually such causes will not be obvious.
- Even scientific researchers frequently fail to acknowledge important rival causes for their findings.
- Do not rely on a single Web page as your only source of causal hypotheses. Check out other sources.
- The certainty of a particular causal claim is inversely related to the number of plausible rival causes.

In the following sections, we explore some implications of these lessons.

Detecting Rival Causes

Locating rival causes is much like being a good detective. When you recognize situations in which rival causes are possible, you should ask questions like these:

Can I think of any other way to interpret the evidence?

What else might have caused this act or these findings?

If I looked at this from another point of view, what important causes might I see?

If this interpretation is incorrect, what other interpretation might make sense?

In the case of studies of humans, try to put yourself in the position of a participant in the study. Would you have certain expectations that would bias your behavior? Would you feel a need to please the researcher? What would it be like to complete the questionnaire or survey? If you were to behave like the research participants, what might cause you to do so?

As you try to generate rival causes, try to blind yourself to the author's interpretation and see whether you can construct your own. Another option is to check other websites and library resources to see whether others have responded to the research. For example, you might type in key words matching the major concepts in the study, seeking links to other sites that discuss the same issues. The more familiar you become with an issue, the easier it will be to generate rival causes.

Rival Causes and Scientific Research

An important quality of scientific research is that it uses systematic procedures to try to eliminate rival causes. That is why you see frequent reference to terms like "control groups" and "randomly assigned." In fact, certain kinds of careful research greatly limit the number of rival causes.

Human behavior, however, is very complex, and even the best research usually fails to eliminate *all* important rival causes. If that's the case, what should you do when websites use research findings to prove that one causes another? Try to find out as much as you can about the research procedures used to obtain the findings that support the hypothesis; then try to identify rival causes that might explain the findings. The more plausible rival causes there are, the less faith you should have in the hypothesis favored by the communicator.

Confusing Causation with Association

We have an inherent tendency to "see" events that are associated, or "go together," as events that cause one another. That is, we conclude that because characteristic X (e.g., early childhood abuse) is associated with characteristic Y (e.g., having an eating disorder), X causes Y.

When we think this way, however, we are often very wrong! Usually, the tendency of the condition of X and the condition of Y to "go together" can be explained in several different ways. Consider an example:

> A recent study reported that "hostility hurts women's health." The researchers studied women over a 31-year period and found that those who were high in hostility at ages 21, 27, and 43 experienced more illness at age 52 than women who were low in hostility. Illness included everything from colds to serious illness. The researchers hypothesized that anger may release stress hormones or impair immunity.

Should women who are high in hostility worry about their physical health? Not yet. First they should consider four potential explanations for the research findings.

> *Explanation 1:* X is a cause of Y. (Hostility does indeed impair women's health; perhaps it stresses their immune system.)
> *Explanation 2:* Y is a cause of X. (Being in poor health may make women feel hostile.)
> *Explanation 3:* X and Y are associated because of a third factor, Z. (Perhaps both hostility and poor health are caused by poor health-related behaviors, such as smoking and lack of exercise, or by stressful life events.)

70

Explanation 4: X and Y influence each other. (Perhaps feeling hostile weakens one's immune system, and in turn, a weaker immune system makes one feel tired, and this makes one feel more hostile.)

Remember: Association or correlation does not prove causation! When an author relies on an association between characteristics to support a particular explanation, always ask, "Are there other causes that explain the association?"

Explaining Specific Events or Acts

Why did President Clinton become sexually involved with a White House intern? What caused the downfall of the Dallas Cowboys in 1999? What caused the stock market to grow far beyond the experts' expectations in 1999?

Like our question about reasons for the Columbine killings, these questions seek the causes of a particular event. Thus far, scientific research has not uncovered general laws powerful enough to explain such specific events. Instead, those seeking understanding frequently search the past for clues. For several reasons, such a search makes us highly susceptible to errors of reasoning. Several of these reasons are especially important to remember.

First, as we saw in the Columbine situation, so many different explanations for the same event can "make sense." Second, how we explain events is greatly influenced by social and political forces, as well as by individual psychological forces. For example, liberals might view the causes of homosexuality differently than conservatives, and feminists might view the causes of anorexia much differently than physicians.

Also, a common bias is the *fundamental attribution error,* in which we overestimate the importance of personality traits relative to situational factors in interpreting the behavior of others. We tend to see the cause of other people's behavior as coming from inside (their personal characteristics) rather than from outside (situational forces). So, for example, when someone shows up late for a date, we're likely to initially view the lateness as being due to the person's tendency to procrastinate or be inconsiderate. However, we should also consider the role of unforeseen situational circumstances, such as car trouble, heavy traffic, or unanticipated company. Consider how differently you would consider the causes of the Columbine shootings if you believed that such acts were usually the result of situational factors than if you believed that they were caused by some kind of evil inside of the person.

Evaluating Rival Causes

The more plausible the rival causes that you identify, the less faith you can have in the initial cause suggested, at least until you can consider further evidence. As a critical thinker, you should assess how each explanation fits the available evidence as well as other knowledge you are aware of, trying to be sensitive to your personal biases. You need to be particularly suspicious when the *only* evidence backing up a cause is post hoc (after the fact) reasoning. We encourage you to add to your list of possible causes by checking multiple Internet sites whose authors are likely to differ in values, perspectives, and political orientations. Then try to determine which of these causes best fits the evidence.

Chapter 13

Political Science and the Internet

The Contestable Nature of Research in Political Science

Whenever you conduct political research on the Internet you will come across conflicting claims. For example, if you wonder about whether Social Security will be around when you retire, you may want to look at some of the many proposals for keeping this program solvent long into the future. The Cato Institute (**http://www.cato.org**) declares that Social Security is a bad deal for everyone and should be replaced by private investment. The Heritage Foundation (**http://www.heritage.org**) suggests that citizens be allowed to partially withdraw from Social Security to finance private investments that would ensure their future retirements. The Century Foundation (**http://www.tcf.org**) claims that Social Security is solvent until 2037 and needs only minor changes to prepare for problems after that year. Whom should you believe? Why do these equally sincere and equally informed policy groups advocate such starkly different viewpoints? Answers to important political questions are not as easy to come by as the public thinks.

Should you continue to search for the RIGHT page about the future of Social Security? If you searched until you found the RIGHT page, you would probably reach retirement first. Different perspectives, values, assumptions, and beliefs shape information, and there is rarely one RIGHT answer. Instead of looking for someone to give you the RIGHT answer, you need to evaluate the information you read and decide which claims seem most credible.

Politics is so complex that definitive research studies are rare. In fact, for most questions, many research studies must be conducted before there can be much convergence on an answer; and in many cases, the more research that is conducted, the more questions that get raised. To complicate matters further, very little of the "research" you will find on the Internet will satisfy generally accepted scientific standards.

Political scientists approach research questions in diverse ways, and their results and interpretations of those results quite often differ. Because of this, there is much debate about just what research results mean. For example, the number of corporate Political Action Committees (PACs) has increased tremendously in the last two decades, while the number of labor PACs has hardly increased at all. What does this mean for the allocation of influence in the political system? Does it mean that corporate interests now dominate labor interests in political influence? Does it mean labor has taken another strategy in achieving their political objectives? Much of the political information that you access from the Net will be greatly influenced by which perspective the author or site sponsor embraces. Political think tanks produce mountains of research every year and, although some are non-partisan, much of their research confirms the think tank's ideological perspectives.

One strength of the discipline of political science is that it emphasizes the desirability of supporting claims about political behavior with empirical research evidence. It is a field that tries to counter the kind of arguments that the Internet encourages by its openness to all points of view—from radical political groups to casual observers of current political events. Political scientists stress the question, What is your evidence? The critical thinker must be able to separate political rhetoric from political science. Political resources that combine factual data and political analysis can blur the line between authoritative information and political advocacy. You must make your own decisions about what to believe by applying your critical-thinking skills.

Research About the Use of the Internet for Learning Political Science

As more information with potential relevance to political science becomes available online, the academic value of the Internet grows. This growth is evidenced by the fact that many textbook publishers now produce supplements and guides to the Internet for political science instructors and their students. Consequently, some instructors have incorporated the Internet in their classroom, thereby surely changing the face of higher education. According to Kandis Steele, "Technology has completely altered the way we think, plan, teach and communicate with our students."[1]

The American Political Science Association (**http://www.apsanet.org**) publishes an online newsletter entitled "Information Technology and Politics" (**http://www.apsanet.org/about/sections/section18.cfm**). This site promotes research on various instructional technologies and their applications in the classroom and distance learning. Several studies have demonstrated that students learn as well over the Internet as they do in the traditional classroom. Michael Gizzi, for example, argues the use of information technology doesn't significantly reduce learning.[2] Research by Charles Kennedy studied the effects

---

[1] Dr. Kandis Steele, "Connecting Political Science and Technology," paper prepared for delivery at the 1999 Annual Meeting of the American Political Science Association, Atlanta, Ga., September 2-5, 1999.

[2] Michael C. Gizzi, "Designing, Developing, and Implementing Internet Courses: Trials and Tribulations of Teaching American Government on the Web," paper prepared for delivery at the 1999 Annual Meeting of the American Political Science Association, Atlanta, Ga., September 2-5, 1999

of technology and team-based teaching on classroom simulations.[3] He found that these methods "can enhance cooperative learning, problem solving, and critical thinking."

Enthusiasm for use of the Internet and other instructional technologies is not shared by everyone. Michael Margolis predicts that traditional colleges and universities will combine in yet unknown ways with private business to produce educational experiences that do not require expensive tenured faculty. According to Margolis, "Inexorably, the strategic logic of corporate management of the higher education market leads to ending professorial tenure as we know it."

Important Websites for Political Science

There are presently thousands of websites providing information relevant to the study of politics. Some are general and cover virtually the entire field; others are restricted to more specific corners of political science.

The University of Michigan maintains "Political Science Resources on the Web" (**http://www.lib.umich.edu/govdocs/polisci.html**), with dozens of pages categorized by subfields and types of information. If you can't find what you want at their site, one of their pages will link you to dozens of other megasites that focus on politics and political science. The other end of the spectrum provides narrowly-focused resources of greatest interest to academic political scientists. "PROceedings" (Political Research Online, **http://pro.harvard.edu**) provides access to conference papers written by and for political scientists. These papers can be very useful to students of political science, but are hardly noticed outside of the discipline.

The subfields of political science address very different subject matter and therefore few sites are important to all of them. American government is so well represented on the Web that finding your way around is easy if you know where to start.

The best entry to the federal government is at the White House website (**http://www.whitehouse.gov**). The "Interactive Citizens' Handbook" (**http://www.whitehouse.gov/government/handbook**) and "First G o v " (**http://www.firstgov.gov**) are especially useful for finding agencies within the bureaucracy.

The information available on Congress in particular is staggering. Aside from the House of Representatives (**http://www.house.gov**) and Senate (**http://www.senate.gov**) sites, several others provide information about our

---

[3]Charles L Kennedy, "Distance Learning Ventures," paper prepared for delivery at the 1999 Annual Meeting of the American Political Science Association, Atlanta, Ga., September 2-5, 1999.

legislators. "Thomas" (**http://thomas.loc.gov**) is the Library of Congress site with information on bills, committee assignments, and the Congressional Record.

The Clerk of the House (**http://clerkweb.house.gov**) provides historical information and explains the way the Congress functions today. "Congress.Org" (**http://congress.org**) provides a format for constituents to reach their representatives. A biographical directory listing every person that has every served in Congress may be found at **http://bioguide.congress.gov**. More information about members of Congress that constituents should know, What is their background? Where did they raise their campaign funds? Where do they stand on the issues? What is their voting record?, may be found at the Public Citizen website (**http://www.citizen.org/congress**). American political websites outside of the government have also thrived on the Internet. Political parties, interest groups, the media, and think tanks have established Web presences.

The subfield of comparative politics has the advantage of having hundreds of countries producing thousands of websites. English-speaking scholars are fortunate in that the American origins and early dominance of the Internet means that English-language websites frequently accompany native-language websites. The downside of such access to worldwide resources is finding them in the crowd. An indirect, but surprisingly effective, strategy is to visit the country's virtual embassy. "The Electronic Embassy" (**http://www.embassy.org/**) has links to all of the foreign embassies in Washington, D.C., that host websites. These websites almost always provide links to that country's English-language websites. Another source for information on foreign governments is the United Nations website at **http://www.un.org**.

International relations is a subfield that has a strong identity beyond the American political science community. The International Studies Association (**http://www.isanet.org**) provides links to other international academic organizations, but the international governmental and non-governmental organizations are best found through the WWW Virtual Library (**http://www.vlib.org/**). "The International Affairs Resources" (**http://www.etown.edu/vl/**) of the WWW Virtual Library has a gateway with over 2200 links to websites related to international relations.

Public policy analysis (at least American policy) is easily accessible on the Web. Numerous traditional think tanks and less-established websites provide policy analysis and position papers on all current policy issues. One of the best ways to find out what these groups have to say is through the "Speakout.com Issues Library" (**http://www.policy.com**). The library has abstracts and links to policy analysis and position papers arranged by policy issues. If you want to find specific policy groups, you can find liberal groups among the "Electronic Policy Network" (**http://epn.org**) and conservative policy groups at the Heritage Foundation's "Policy Experts" (**http://www.policyexperts.org**).

Political theory is perhaps the least well-represented political science subfield on the Internet. The graphics, data, and current events that are important to much of the discipline are not quite as relevant to political theory. The best place to find out what is available is through "Foundations in Political Theory" (**http://www.political-theory.org**), sponsored by the political theory section of the American Political Science Association. Look under "Online texts," but you will actually find more by looking under "Theorists" and using these links as starting points to find biographies and more online texts than are listed at this site.

Political methodology has some resources available on the Internet that students may find useful. The latest and most technical resources are available from the Society for Political Methodology (**http://web.polmeth.ufl.edu**). Here you can find articles, data sets, and links to sites that explain the most recent statistical methods. Students may find Richard Tucker's "Political Science Research Resources" (**http://www.vanderbilt.edu/~rtucker/polisci/**) more accessible for someone just getting involved in quantitative methods and formal theory.

Searching for the Right Search Engine

When you're searching for information, if you aren't sure where to start, a good place is usually a search engine of some kind. What you find will depend on the particular search engine, so it is helpful to understand the range of search tools available. Categories of search tools include: hierarchical indexes, standard search engines, alternative search engines, meta search engines, and databases. In a hierarchical index, people trained to categorize information, such as librarians, examine websites and put them in categories and subcategories. Such categorizing makes it easier for you to find relevant sites; for example, if you browse within Yahoo (**http://www.yahoo.com**), you will find a social science category, and under that category you will find "Political Science" and subcategories such as the following: "Political Theory," "International Relations," and "Public Policy." Several other, more academic, hierarchical indexes are: BUBL Link (**http://www.bubl.ac.uk/link**) and Infomine (**http://infomine.ucr.edu**).

Unlike hierarchical indexes, standard search engines send out "robots" or "spiders" to search the Web and index the pages in each site they encounter. Each engine then uses some system to rank pages, such as calculating the frequency and placement of your keywords on a page. The search engine puts the pages that get the highest score at the top of the list of results. It is usually best to avoid standard search engines when you have a very broad subject, such as "elections" or "president," and instead focus on a few relevant sites from a hierarchical index. Standard search engines include: AltaVista (**http://www.altavista.com**), Excite (**http://www.excite.com**), Go.com (**http://infoseek.go.com**), and HotBot (**http://hotbot.lycos.com**).

Alternative search engines try to improve the search process over standard engines by using different approaches to the ranking and sorting of the pages.

Northern Light (**http://www.northernlight.com**), for instance, ranks Web pages as a standard search engine does, but rather than displaying all findings in a single listing, it sorts pages into categories and groups the results into folders. As an example, a search for "political parties" creates 14 folders, with names such as: "Search Current News," "Special Collection Documents," "National Government," and "Elections." Such arrangement of material can help you determine which groups of pages are most likely to be relevant to your needs.

Another alternative engine, Google (**http://www.google.com**), first matches up your keywords to the pages it has collected in its index, then ranks each page based on how many other pages link to it—and how many link to those pages in turn. Thus, it puts pages with the most links at the top of its list.

Oingo (**http://www.oingo.com**) conducts a "conceptual search" to make sure that it understands your request. Ask it to search for "Supreme Court," for example, and it will ask you to choose between "U.S. Supreme Court Decisions" and "State Supreme Courts." Once you select "U.S. Supreme Court Decisions," Oingo will display "More General Topics" and "Web hits." Under "More General Topics," for example, you will see "Federal Courts in the United States," and under "Web hits," you will see such sites as "Findlaw: Supreme Court Decisions" and "FLITE: Supreme Court Decisions 1937-1975." The site combines a hierarchical index and a search engine.

A fun, rather different, kind of search engine is Ask Jeeves (**http://www.askjeeves.com**). Instead of entering keywords, you type a question in plain English. You might ask, for example, "Who was president in 1863?" Ask Jeeves has recorded thousands of questions that users have asked it, and has found websites that answer those questions. After receiving your question, Ask Jeeves first scans its database of questions and answers and then tries to match questions it "thinks" you are trying to ask with your question. One of the options Jeeves returns is "Where can I find information about U.S. President Abraham Lincoln?" In this particular case, you will find ten matches at About.com and several at other search engines.

Search engines that search other engines are called meta search engines. Other popular ones are Dogpile (**http://www.dogpile.com**) and MetaCrawler (**http://www.metacrawler.com**). The underlying rationale is that no single search engine can scan all sites. A drawback to these sites is that they need to use search strategies that can be followed by all of the search engines; thus, they're usually not the best choice for complex searches. They are, however, an excellent place to search for obscure names and terms.

The above search tools will eventually get you to most of the discipline-specific sites that we previously mentioned. Regardless how you choose to search for information, you will get the best results if you know what information you need and become familiar with the advantages and disadvantages of different kinds of searches.

Thinking Critically About Political Information on the Internet

In this section we apply the critical-thinking questions that the book has been emphasizing by critically evaluating some information from a current political debate. The purpose of this discussion is to provide a brief example of a coherent application of the diverse critical-thinking steps. We suggest that you use the discussion as a check on your understanding of the previous chapters. Would you have asked the same questions? Would you have formed similar answers? Do you feel better able to judge the worth of someone's reasoning?

Let's begin with a question checklist:
*   What argument does the site present?
*   What is the source of the information?
*   How dependable is the authority that provided the information?
*   What does the information mean?
*   What are the primary value assumptions of the site?
*   What is the quality of the evidence?
*   Are there rival causes for the results described at the site?
*   What important information is omitted?

The Example

Let's assume that you have developed an interest in alternate forms of taxation. One commonly proposed alternative to the current system is a proportional tax, often referred to as the "flat tax," which proposes that all income be taxed at the same low rate with no deductions or loopholes. You decide to use the Web to check out whether such a plan has any merit. If you click on to Google (**http://www.google.com**) and use the keyword "flat tax," you will find several potentially relevant sites. Let's assume that you click onto one that looks pretty relevant, such as "The Flat Tax Calculator." At that site you find a set of questions about your income, marital status, and dependent children. By filling out this information your federal taxes are calculated as if The Freedom and Fairness Restoration Act were to become law. There are also links to the text of the proposed law and research studies. If you click/select "Congressman Dick Armey's Home Page" (U.S. Representative Dick Armey at **http://armey.house.gov**), you can read an article called "How Taxes Corrupt." Click on the Flattax.gov link, then the Details link, and finally the Armey Studies option. You now have a Web page of information to critically evaluate. The website reports the following:

Economists have produced countless studies that show how our uneven, complex tax code costs our economy billions of dollars in higher compliance costs and reduced efficiency. But perhaps worse than the economic cost is the effect our arbitrary tax system has had on Washington's political culture. Because our tax system lacks any coherent principle—such as taxing all income one time at the same rate—tax policy has evolved into a free-for-all for special interests.

Let's now ask questions to help us decide what to make of this information.

What Argument Does the Site Present?
The author is clearly interested in the issue of whether the current tax system is unfairly biased toward special interests. The article includes research results to support the following conclusion:

> Congress has used the tax code to pick winners and losers and hand out special favors. As a result, the public interest has been short-changed while the lobbying industry has flourished. Steve Forbes is right when he charges that the current income tax code is the chief source of political corruption in the nation's capital.

What are the reasons supporting the conclusion? In this case, the reasons are in the form of data about lobbyists and changes in the tax code. The main reason (evidence) supporting the conclusion is the observation that the number of changes in the tax code has increased during the same time as the number of lobbyists has increased.

What Is the Source of the Information?
The fact that the site address ends in ".gov" suggests that the site probably is sponsored by some part of the government, in this case Representative Dick Armey. Click on to the "details" page and you will discover that the purpose of the site is to advocate for the replacement of the current tax system with a flat tax plan devised by Representative Armey and Senator Richard Shelby. While Armey is probably very sincere in his opinions, he is also an advocate for an alternative to the current system.

There also is a "Third Party Studies" link, which presents several studies and articles from ostensibly neutral viewpoints. Because the sources are almost exclusively from conservative authors and groups, you should be concerned about the possibility of selective biases in choosing studies for this source.

How Dependable Is the Authority Who Provided the Information?
In addition to examining the source, we should also take a close look at the particular authorities that provided the Web page containing the research study. We first need to check the format in which the article was published. Was it serious scholarship in an edited professional journal, or was it in another form? The byline states that the article is reprinted from *The Wall Street Journal*, a conservative, but not overtly biased, source of news and analysis. The author, Dick Armey himself, is only credited at the bottom. Thus the article is not from the staff of *The Wall Street Journal*, but is apparently an Op-Ed article submitted by Armey. The observation that Armey is the author of the article and an advocate for an alternative tax system should not lead us to conclude the article

is necessarily biased. We should look deeper into the merits of the analysis presented in the article.

What Does the Information Mean?

We would certainly want to know more about the specific meaning of "pick winners and losers" and "chief source of corruption" in order to get a clearer picture of just what is being argued. We should ask, Just who does and does not receive the tax breaks passed by Congress? And, How does lobbying corrupt legislators? In fact, we should ask, What are the other sources of corruption and how do they compare to tax code lobbying? Information about who does and does not receive tax breaks is abundant but not presented here at all. The author plainly states that lobbyists corrupt legislators but fails to explain how they do it. What constitutes corruption? The author doesn't seem to imply illegal activity, so what lesser level of corruption does he believe exists?

What Are the Primary Value Assumptions of the Site?

Because this is both a descriptive argument, focusing on the way the world is, and a prescriptive argument, what it ought to be, value assumdtions are clearly present. Even if the charges of the corrupting influence of tax breaks were proven to be true and all tax breaks eliminated, it is less than self-evident that many lobbyists would pack their bags and stop trying to influence legislation. The author assumes that this would be the outcome without indicating how it would come about. As a conservative, the author does not even consider liberal alternatives to the corrupting influence of lobbyists such as public financing of congressional campaigns, limiting campaign funds, and eliminating PAC contributions. We don't know that any of these liberal alternatives would be more effective or even as effective, but Armey's value assumptions eliminate these alternatives without consideration.

What Is the Quality of the Evidence?

One strength of the study is that Armey did produce data to back up his arguments. Few politicians feel they need to go beyond anecdotes to support their convictions. The question to ask when confronted with evidence is, *Does the evidence prove what the author says it proves?* Armey demonstrates in a graph that the number of lobbyists and the complexity of the tax code (in words and sections) have increased at similar rates since 1964. The association of lobbyists and tax code complexity is what is known as a correlation. As one variable changes, so does another variable. When we see a robin for the first time spring will soon follow. We cannot conclude that robins cause spring and we cannot, without substantial evidence, conclude that simply increasing the total number of lobbyists produces greater tax code complexity. This is a reasonable hypothesis, but still an unproven hypothesis. It is an even greater stretch to assume that tax code complexity is evidence of corruption.

Are There Rival Causes for the Results Described on the Site?

Effective political arguments should recognize and address alternative explanations for the descriptions and prescriptions they offer. Armey argues that

81

lobbying corrupted legislators in some way to induce them to create tax breaks for special interests. Are these lobbyists without merit in seeking tax breaks? Farmers' organizations seeking special treatment don't go to urban legislators; they go to legislators who represent farmers. Is the legislator in this instance corrupted by the lobbyists or merely representing constituents? Is the tax code corrupting the legislators or is it caused by campaign contributions by special interests? If it is the latter, no degree of tax reform will eliminate the supposed corruption. The conclusion is not that Armey is wrong, merely that the range of alternatives he considers is too narrow.

What Significant Information Is Omitted?
Our prior questioning suggests important omitted information, such as definitions of tax breaks and corruption. Also, it would be useful to know how lobbyists corrupt legislators. Armey may assume that campaign contributions by special interests elicit favors from legislators, and many political scientists would support this assumption. Some political scientists, however, conclude that many campaign contributions are coerced out of PACs by the legislators themselves. The path of influence and coercion is uncertain and cannot be assumed.

Conclusion
This is just an example of one study on a topic that has been argued by researchers and political advocates in recent years. By approaching it as a critical thinker, you should have a better sense of its strengths and its weaknesses, what it highlights and what it hides, and how much you should be influenced by it. If you had encountered this study, a useful next step would have been to check out several other websites on this topic to get a good sense of the diversity of information that is available. It is quite likely you would find authors on the Web that would strongly disagree about the influence of lobbyists over tax policy.

Appendix A

Documenting Your Electronic Sources

Copyright laws came into effect when people started realizing that income could be made by selling their words. In an era dubbed "The Age of Information," knowledge and words are taking on more significance than ever. Laws requiring writers to document or give credit to the sources of their information, while evolving, are still in effect.

Various organizations have developed style manuals detailing, among other style matters, how to document sources in their particular disciplines. For writing in English composition and literature, Modern Language Association (MLA) and American Psychological Association (APA) guidelines are the most commonly used, but others, such as those in *The Chicago Manual of Style* (CMS), are available. Always find out from your instructor what style to use in a specific assignment so that you can follow the appropriate guidelines.

For general information on MLA and APA citations, the best print sources are:

> Gibaldi, Joseph. MLA Handbook for Writers of Research Papers. 5th ed. NY: MLA, 1999.

> American Psychological Association. (2001). *Publication Manual of the American Psychological Association* (5th ed.). Washington: APA.

Because the methods of obtaining electronic information are developing so rapidly, printed style manuals have had difficulty in keeping up with the changes and in developing documentation styles for electronic sources. As a result, the most up-to-date information from the MLA and the APA about documenting online sources with URLs can be found on these organizations' websites. This Appendix shows you how to credit your electronic sources based on the information there.

When you cite electronic sources, it is vital to type every letter, number, symbol, and space accurately. Any error makes it impossible to retrieve your source. Since electronic sources tend to be transitory, printing a hard copy of your sources will make it easier for you to cite accurately and provide evidence for your documentation. MLA style encloses Internet addresses and URLs (Uniform Resource Locators) in angle brackets < >. If you see them around an address, do not use them as part of the address when you attempt to retrieve the source. APA style does not enclose URLs.

Modern Language Association (MLA) Style Guidelines

These guidelines follow the documentation style authorized by the Modern Language Association for electronic sources. Web sources are documented in basically the same way as traditional sources. According to the MLA website, the following items should be included if they are available:

1. Name of the author, editor, compiler, or translator of the source (if available and relevant), reversed for alphabetizing and followed by an abbreviation, such as ed., if appropriate
2. Title of a poem, short story, article, or similar short work within a scholarly project, database, or periodical (in quotation marks); or title of a posting to a discussion list or forum (taken from the subject line and put in quotation marks), followed by the description Online posting
3. Title of a book (underlined)
4. Name of the editor, compiler, or translator of the text (if relevant and if not cited earlier), preceded by the appropriate abbreviation, such as ed.
5. Publication information for any print version of the source
6. Title of the scholarly project, database, periodical, or professional or personal site (underlined); or, for a professional or personal site with no title, a description such as Homepage
7. Name of the editor of the scholarly project or database (if available)
8. Version number of the source (if not part of the title) or, for a journal, the volume number, issue number, or other identifying number
9. Date of electronic publication, of the latest update, or of posting
10. For a posting to a discussion list or forum, the name of the list or forum
11. The number range or total number of pages, paragraphs, or other sections, if they are numbered
12. Name of any institution or organization sponsoring or associated with the website
13. Date when the researcher accessed the source
14. Electronic address, or URL, of the source (in angle brackets)

Examples:

Book

Shaw, Bernard. <u>Pygmalion</u>. 1912. Bartleby Archive. 6
    Mar. 1998 <http://www.columbia.edu/acis/
    bartleby/shaw/>.

Poem

Carroll, Lewis. "Jabberwocky." 1872. 6 Mar. 1998.
    <http://www.jabberwocky.com/carroll/jabber/
    jabberwocky.html>.

Article in a Journal

Rehberger, Dean. "The Censoring of Project #17:
Hypertext Bodies and Censorship." *Kairos* 2.2
(Fall 1997): 14 secs. 6 Mar. 1998 <http://
english.ttu.edu/kairos/2.2/index_f.html>.

Article in a Magazine

Viagas, Robert, and David Lefkowitz. "Capeman Closing
Mar. 28." *Playbill* 5 Mar. 1998. 6 Mar. 1998
<http://www1.playbill.com/cgi-bin/plb/news?cmd
=show&code=30763>.

Article in a Newspaper

Sandomir, Richard. "Yankees Talk Trades in Broadcast
Booth." *New York Times on the Web* 4 Dec. 2001. 5
Dec. 2001 <http://www.nytimes.com/pages/
business/media/index.html>.

Article in a Reference Database

"Jupiter." Britannica Online. Vers. 97.1.1 Mar. 1997.
Encyclopaedia Britannica. 29 Mar. 1998 <http://
www.eb.com:180>.

Posting to a Discussion List

Grumman, Bob. "Shakespeare's Literacy." Online
posting. 6 Mar. 1998. Deja News. <humanities.
lit.author>.

Scholarly Project

*Voice of the Shuttle: Web Page for Humanities
Research*. Ed. Alan Liu. Mar. 1998. U of
California Santa Barbara. 8 Mar. 1998
<http://humanitas.ucsb.edu/>.

Professional Site

The Nobel Foundation Official Website. The Nobel
Foundation. 28 Feb. 1998 <http://www.nobel.se/>.

Personal Site

Thiroux, Emily. Home page. 7 Mar. 1998
<http://academic.csubak.edu/home/acadpro/
departments/english/engthrx.htmlx>.

Government or Institutional Site

Zebra Mussels in Vermont. Homepage. State of Vermont
Agency of Natural Resources. 3 May 1998 <http://
www.anr.state.vt.us/dec/waterq/smcap.htm>.

Synchronous Communications (such as MOOs, MUDs, and IRCs)

Ghostly Presence. Group Discussion. telnet 16 Mar.
1997 <moo.du.org:8000/80anon/anonview/1
4036#focus>.

Gopher Sites

Banks, Vickie, and Joe Byers. "EDTECH." 18 Mar. 1997
<gopher://ericyr.syr.edu:70/00/Listservs/EDTECH/
README>.

FTP (File Transfer Protocol) Sites

U.S. Supreme Court directory. 6 Mar. 1998
<ftp://ftp.cwru.edu/U.S.Supreme.Court/>.

Online work of art

Van Gogh, Vincent. The Olive Trees. 1889. Museum of
Modern Art, New York. 5 Dec. 2001 <http://
www.moma.org/docs/collection/paintsculpt/
recent/c463.htm>.

Online interview

Plaxco, Jim. Interview. Planetary Studies Foundation.
Oct. 1992. 5 Dec. 2001 <http://www.planets.org>.

Online film or film clip

Columbus, Chris, dir. Harry Potter and the Sorcerer's
Stone. Trailer. Warner Brothers, 2001. 5 Dec.
2001 <http://hollywood.com>.

Electronic television or radio program

Chayes, Sarah. "Concorde." All Things Considered.
Natl. Public Radio. 26 July 2000. 7 Dec. 2001
<http://www.npr.com/programs/atc/archives>.

Synchronous communication

Author's last name, First name. Identifying label.
"Title of work." xx Month 20xx. Name of forum.
xx Month 20xx. <Telnet://lingua.networkname>.

Generally follow the guidelines for other online citations, modifying them wherever necessary, but always provide as much information as possible. Some cited material will require identifying labels (e.g., Interview or Online posting), but such labels should be neither underlined nor set within quotation marks. When documenting synchronous communications that are posted in MOO (multiuser domain, object oriented) and MUD (multiuser domain) forums, name the speaker or speakers; describe the event; provide the date of the event and the name of the forum (e.g., linguaMOO); and cite the date of access as well as the network name (including the prefix Telnet://).

Work from an Online Service
```
Author's last name, First name. Publication. 20xx.
     Internet Provider name. xx Month 20xx. Keyword:
     Name.
```

Or

```
Last name, First name. Publication. 20xx. Internet
     Provider name. xx Month 20xx. Path: Name; Name;
     Name.
```

```
Brash, Stephen B. "Bioprospecting the Public Domain."
     Cultural Anthropology 14.4 (1999): 535—56.
     ProQuest Direct. Teaneck Public Library,
     Teaneck, NJ. 7 Dec. 1999 <http://proquest.
     umi.com>.
```

Or

```
Dutton, Gail. "Greener Pigs." Popular Science 255.5
     (1999): 38—39. ProQuest Direct. Teaneck Public
     Library, Teaneck, NJ. 7 Dec. 1999 <http://
     proquest.umi.com>.
```

For works that have been accessed through an online service, either through a library service (e.g., ProQuest Direct or Lexis-Nexis) or through one of the large Internet providers (e.g., America Online), you may not know the URL of the source. In such cases, cite the keyword or path that led to the source, if applicable, and separate each individual item in the path with a semicolon; the keyword or path will be the last item in the citation. For sources accessed through library services, as above, cite the name of the service, the name of the library, the date you assessed the material, and the URL of the service's homepage. If you also know the name of the database used, include that information (underlined) before the name of the online service.

American Psychological Association (APA) Style Guidelines

The most recent (5th) edition of the *Publication Manual of the American Psychological Association* includes general guidelines for citing electronic sources, and the APA has published specific examples for documenting Web sources on its Web page. Go to:

http://www.apastyle.org/elecre.html

In general, document these sources as you do traditional sources, giving credit to the author and including the title and date of publication. Include as much information as possible to help your reader to be able to retrieve the information. Any sources that are not generally available to your readers should be documented within the body of your writing as a personal communication but not included in your reference list. Such sources include material from listservs, newsgroups, Internet relay chats (IRCs), MOOs, MUDs, and e-mail.

According to information at the website for the American Psychological Association entitled "How to Cite Information From the World Wide Web," all references begin with the same information that would be provided for a printed source (or as much of that information as possible). The Web information is then placed at the end of the reference. It is important to use the "Retrieved from" and the date because documents on the Web may change in content, move, or be removed from a site altogether. To cite a website in text (but not a specific document), it's sufficient to give the address (e.g., http://www.apa.org) there. No reference entry is needed.

Use the following guidelines to include a source in your reference list:

```
Name of author [if given]. (Publication date) [in
    parentheses]. Title of the article [following
    APA guidelines for capitalization]. Title of
    periodical or electronic text [italicized].
    Volume number and/or pages [if any]. Retrieved
    [include the date here] from the World Wide Web:
    [include the URL here, and do not end with a
    period]
```

Examples:

Journal Article
Fine, M. A. & Kurdek, L. A. (1993, November).
Reflections on determining authorship credit and
authorship order on faculty-student
collaborations. *American Psychologist*, 48.11,
1141-1147. Retrieved March 6, 1998 from the
World Wide Web: http://www.apa.org/journals/
amp/kurdek.html

Newspaper Article
Murray, B. (1998, February). Email bonding with your
students. *APA Monitor* [Newspaper, selected
stories online]. Retrieved March 6, 1998 from
the World Wide Web: http://www.apa.org/monitor/
bond.html

World Wide Web site
Williams, Scott. (1996, June 14). Back to school
with the quilt. *AIDS Memorial Quilt Website*.
Retrieved June 14, 1996, from http://www.
aidsquilt.org/newsletter/stoires/backto.html

File transfer protocol (FTP), telnet, or gopher site
Altar, T.W. (1993). *Vitamin B12 and vegans*. Retrieved
May 28, 1996, from ftp://ftp.cs.yle.edu

King, Jr., M.L. (1963, August 28). I have a dream
[speech]. Retrieved January 2, 1996, from
telnet://ukanaix.cc.ukans.edu

Synchronous communications (MOO, MUD, IRC)
Harnack, A. (1996, April 4). Words [Group
discussion]. Retrieved April 5, 1996, from
telnet://moo.du.org/port=8888

Web discussion forum
Holden, J.B. (2001, January 2). The failure of higher
education [Formal discussion initiation].
Message posted to http://ifets.mtu.edu/archives

Listserv (electronic mailing list)

Weston, Heather (2002, June 12). Re: Registration schedule now available. Message posted to the Chamberlain Kronsage dormitory electronic mailing list, archived at http://listserv. registrar.uwsp.edu/archives/62.html

Newsgroup

Hotgirl (2002, January 12). Dowsing effort fails. Message posted to news://alt.science.esp3/html

Appendix B
Glossary

Access Provider A company that provides access to the Internet or a private network for a fee. (See Internet Service Provider.)

Agent A type of software program that can be directed to automatically search the Internet or perform a specific function on behalf of a user. Spiders and worms, which roam the Internet, are the most common types of agents.

Anchor An HTML tag used by a Web page author to designate a connection between a word in the text and a link to another page. (See HTML, Tag, and Link.)

AVI This stands for Audio/Video Interleaved. It is a Microsoft Corporation format for encoding video and audio for digital transmission.

Backbone The main network cable or link in a large Internet.

Bandwidth The capacity of a network line to carry user requests. Network lines such as a T1 are larger (have a higher bandwidth) and can carry more information than a lower bandwidth line such as an ISDN or a modem connection. (See ISDN and Modem.)

Bookmark A list of URLs saved within a browser. The user can edit and modify the bookmark list to add and delete URLs as the user's interests change. Bookmark is a term used by Netscape to refer to the user's list of URLs; Hotlist is used by Mosaic for the same purpose. (See Hotlist and URL.)

Browser A software program that is used to view and browse information on the Internet. Browsers are also referred to as clients. (See Client.)

Bulletin Board Service (BBS) An electronic bulletin board, it is sometimes referred to as a BBS. Information on a BBS is posted to a computer where people can access, read, and comment on it. A BBS may or may not be connected to the Internet. Some are accessible by modem dial-in only.

Cache A section of memory set aside to store information that is commonly used by the computer or by an active piece of software. Most browsers will create a cache for commonly-accessed images. An example might be the images that are common to the user's homepage. Retrieving images from the cache is much quicker than downloading the images from the original source each time they are required.

91

Chat room A site that allows real-time person-to-person interactions.

Client A software program used to view information from remote computers. Clients function in a Client-Server information exchange model. This term may also be loosely applied to the computer that is used to request information from the server. (See Server.)

Computer Virus A program designed to infect a computer and possibly cause problems within the infected system. Viruses are typically passed from user to user through the exchange of an infected file. Numerous virus checkers or scanners are available to help you identify and inoculate your system against viruses.

Compressed file A file or document that has been compacted to save memory space so that it can be easily and quickly transferred through the Internet.

Cookie A small piece of information given temporarily to your Web browser by a Web server. The cookie is used to record information about you or your browsing behavior for later use by the server. For example, when you visit an online bookstore, a cookie will probably be passed to your browser to record book selections you make for purchase.

Cyberspace This refers to the "world" of computers. It was coined by William Gibson in the novel *Neuromancer*.

Dial-Up Account This refers to having registered permission to access a remote computer by which you are allowed to connect through a modem.

Domain One of the different subsets of the Internet. The suffix found on the host name of an Internet server defines its domain. For example, the host name for Prentice Hall, the publisher of this book, is www.prenhall.com. The last part, .COM, indicates that Prentice Hall is a part of the commercial domain. Other domains include .MIL for military, .EDU for education, .ORG for non-profit organizations, .GOV for government organizations, and many more.

Download The process of transferring a file, document, or program from a remote computer to a local computer. (See Upload.)

E-mail The short name for electronic mail. E-mail is sent electronically from one person to another. Some companies have e-mail systems that are not part of the Internet. E-mail can be sent to one person or to many different people.

Encryption A security procedure of coding information to prevent unwanted viewing. Information sent across a computer network is typically disassembled, shipped, and reassembled on the receiving computer. Encrypted information must be decrypted with a special "encryption key" by the receiving party.

Executable File A file or program that can run (execute) by itself and that does not require another program. Some files, such as word processor documents, require an applications program for viewing them.

External Viewer Application Browsers are software applications that enable users to display content distributed on the Web. Web information must be in one of a few specific formats before the browser can display it for the users. An External Viewer Application can be used to view files sent across the Web that cannot be viewed within the browser. These applications are said to be external because they do not operate within the browser. (See Plug-in.)

FAQ This stands for frequently asked questions. A FAQ is a file or document where a moderator or administrator will post commonly asked questions and their answers. Although it is very easy to communicate across the Internet, if you have a question, you should check for the answer in a FAQ first.

Firewall A firewall is a network server that functions to control traffic flow between two separate networks. They are typically used to separate large government and corporate sites from the Internet. Some colleges use firewalls to protect certain areas of their network.

Flame Degrading a person over the Internet is referred to as flaming. Non-verbal communication is not typically possible across a computer network, unless you have a video hookup, so misunderstandings often result. Anonymity of the flamer also contributes to such an exchange because people are more likely to make impolite statements given their physical separation.

FTP This stands for File Transfer Protocol. It is a procedure used to transfer large files and programs from one computer to another. Access to the computer to transfer files may or may not require a password. Some FTP servers are set up to allow public access by anonymous log-on. This process is referred to as Anonymous FTP.

GIF This stands for Graphics Interchange Format. It is a format created by CompuServe to allow electronic transfer of digital images. GIF files are a commonly-used format and can be viewed by both Mac and Windows users.

Gopher A format structure and resource for providing information on the Internet. It was created at the University of Minnesota.

GUI An acronym for Graphical User Interface. Macintosh and Windows operating systems are examples of typical GUIs.

Helper This is software that is used to help a browser view information formats that it couldn't normally view.

Hits This refers to a download request made by a browser to a server. Each file from a website that is requested by the browser is referred to as a hit. A Web page may be composed of numerous file elements and although hit counts are often reported as a measure of popularity, they can be misleading.

Homepage In its specific sense, this refers to a Web document that a browser loads as its central navigational point to browse the Internet. It may also be used to refer to as Web page describing an individual. In the most general sense, it is used to refer to any Web document.

Host Another name for a server computer. (See Server.)

Hotlist This is a list of URLs saved within the Mosaic Web browser. This same list is referred to as a Bookmark within the Netscape Web browser.

HTML This is an abbreviation for HyperText Markup Language, the common language used to write documents that appear on the World Wide Web.

HTTP An abbreviation for HyperText Transport Protocol, the common protocol used to communicate between World Wide Web servers.

Hypertext An embedded connection within a Web page that connects to a site within the viewed Web page or to a different Web page. Web pages use hypertext links to call up documents, images, sounds, and video files. The term hyperlink is a general term that applies to elements on Web pages other than text elements.

Icon This refers to a visual representation of a file or program as it is represented on a typical windows graphic user interface (GUI). For example, Apple uses a trashcan icon to represent the place to put files you want to delete or remove from your computer. Microsoft uses a wastepaper basket.

Internet Relay Chat (IRC) IRC is a network attached to the Internet. It allows users to converse in real time with other individuals. It is not typically a one-on-one conversation. Chat "rooms" are typically a very confusing place for beginners.

Internet Service Provider (ISP) A company that provides Internet access is an ISP. Your ISP might be your school or a company to which you subscribe on a monthly basis.

Intranet This refers to a network of networks that does not have a connection to THE Internet.

ISDN This stands for Integrated Services Digital Network. It is a digital phone line. ISDN service is typically more expensive but also offers customers added features such as a greater bandwidth. (See Bandwidth.)

Java   An object-oriented programming language developed by Sun Microsystems.

JavaScript   A scripting language developed by Netscape in cooperation with Sun Microsystems to add functionality to the basic Web page. It is not as powerful as Java and works primarily from the client side.

JPEG   This stands for Joint Photographic Experts Group. It is one of the common standards for pictures on the Internet.

Local Area Network (LAN)   A LAN is a small or local network, typically within a single building.

Link   A text element or graphic within a document that has an embedded connection to another item. Web pages use links to access documents, images, sounds, and video files from the Internet, other documents on the local Web server, or other content on the Web page. Hyperlink is another name for link.

List Administrator   An individual that monitors or oversees a mailing list. (See Mailing List.)

Login   Generally, this refers to the act of connecting to a network but it may also indicate the need to enter a username or password to access a network or server.

Lurker   An individual who connects to a chat room, bulletin board, or newsgroup and observes the conversation but does not participate.

Mailing List   A functional group of e-mail addresses intended for making group mailings. It is used as a simple bulletin board. Some mailing lists are moderated by an individual and some are automatic. The most common mistake made by people using mailing lists is that they reply to a message and forget that everyone on the list will receive and potentially read their note. This can have embarrassing consequences.

MIME Type   This stands for Multipurpose Internet Mail Extension. It is a standard used to identify files by their extension or suffix. Applications, like your e-mail client, are said to be MIME compliant when they can decode MIME suffixes. (See MOV, MPG, PDF.)

Mirror site   Some sites on the Internet are very popular and under heavy demand by the viewing public and are potentially overloaded with traffic. Mirror sites are exact copies of the original site that help to distribute the traffic load, increasing efficiencies in delivering information.

Modem A modem is a device used to send and receive information across a phone line by your computer. Computers speak digital and telephones speak analog. Essentially, a modem is a translator. Modems are only one kind of device available for connecting your computer to the outside world. Two other methods becoming more common for home use are ISDN and cable.

MOV This stands for movie. It is a file extension for animations and videos in the QuickTime file format.

MPG/MPEG This stands for Motion Picture Experts Group. It is a format for both digital audio and digital video files.

Multimedia As a general definition, multimedia is the presentation of information by multiple media formats, such as words, images, and sound. Today, it's more commonly used to refer to presentations that use a lot of computer technology.

Nettiquette This is a word created to mean Network Etiquette. It is a general list of practices and suggestions to help preserve the peace on the Internet. (See Flame.)

Newsgroup This is the name for the discussion groups that can be on the Usenet. Not all newsgroups are accessible through the Internet. Some are accessible only through a modem connection. (See Usenet.)

Pathname A convention for describing or outlining the location of a file or directory on a host computer. A URL is typically composed of several elements in addition to the pathname. For example, in this URL: http://www.prenhall.com/pubguide/index.html, http:// describes the protocol for a Web server, www.prenhall.com is the name of the host or server, /pubguide/ is the pathname, and index.html is the file name.

PDF This stands for Portable Document Format. It is a file format that allows authors to distribute formatted, high-resolution documents across the Internet. A free viewer, Adobe Acrobat Reader, is required to view PDF documents.

Plug-in This is a resource or program that can be added to a browser to extend its function and capabilities.

QuickTime (QT) A file format developed by Apple Computer so that computers can play digital audio, animation, and video files. (See MOV, MPG.)

Robot An automated program used to search and explore the Internet. Some popular search engines use these programs.

Search Engine An online service or utility that enables users to query and search the Internet for user-defined information. They are typically free services to the user. (See Robot.)

Search String A logical collection of terms or phrases used to descr.
request. Some search engines enable the user to define strings with Book
such as AND, NOT, or OR. (See Search Engine.)

Server A software program used to provide, or serve, information to remo
computers. Servers function in a Client-Server information exchange model.
This term may also be loosely applied to the computer that is used to serve the
information. (See Client.)

Shareware Software that is provided to the public on a try-before-you-buy
basis. Shareware functions on the honor system. Once you've used it for a while,
you are expected to pay a small fee. Two similar varieties of software are
Freeware and Postcardware. Freeware is just that, free for your use and the
owners of Postcardware simply ask you to send them a postcard to thank them
for the product.

Shockwave Shockwave is a plug-in that allows Macromedia programs to be
played on your Web browser. Many learning tools are beginning to be posted to
the Web as Shockwave files. Visit Macromedia's website for more information
and to download the plug-in (http://www.macromedia.com/). (See Plug-in.)

Signature A signature is text that is automatically added to the bottom of
electronic communications such as e-mail or newsgroup postings. A signature
usually lists the name and general information about the person making the
posting. Using a signature means that you don't have to repeatedly type your
name and return information every time you send a note.

Spam The electronic version of junk mail. It also refers to the behavior of
sending or posting a single note to numerous e-mail or newsgroup accounts. It is
considered to be very bad nettiquette.

Stuff The action of compressing a file using the Stuff-It program. This is a
Macintosh format.

Table A specific formatting element found in HTML pages. Tables are used
on HTML documents to visually organize information.

Telnet The process of remotely connecting and using a computer at a distant
location.

Thread This describes a linked series of newsgroup postings. It represents a
conversation stream. Messages posted on active newsgroups are likely to spur
numerous replies each of which can spin off into an independent conversation.
The nature of newsgroups allows a reader to move forward or backward through
a conversation as if moving along a string or thread.

Topic Drift This describes the phenomena observed in many online
conversations, typically chat or newsgroup, where the topic will drift or change
from the original posting.

Upload The process of moving or transferring a document, file, or program from one computer to another computer.

URL An abbreviation for Universal Resource Locator. In its basic sense, it is an address used by people on the Internet to locate documents. URLs have a common format that describes the protocol for information transfer, the host computer address, the path to the desired file, and the name of the file requested.

Usenet A worldwide system of discussion groups, also called newsgroups. There are many thousands of newsgroups, but only some of these are accessible from the Internet.

User Name An ID used as identification on a computer or network. It is a string of alphanumeric characters that may or may not have any resemblance to a user's real name.

Viewer A program used to view data files within or outside a browser. (See External Viewer Application.)

Virtual Reality (VR) A simulation of three-dimensional space on the computer. (See VRML.)

VRML This stands for Virtual Reality Markup Language. It was developed to allow the creation of virtual reality worlds. Your browser may need a specific plug-in to view VRML pages.

WAV This stands for Waveform sound format. It is a Microsoft Corporation format for encoding sound files.

Web (WWW) This stands for the World Wide Web. When loosely applied, this term refers to the Internet and all of its associated incarnations, including Gopher, FTP, HTTP, and others. More specifically, this term refers to a subset of the servers on the Internet that use HTTP to transfer hyperlinked documents in a page-like format.

Webmaster This is the general title given to the administrator of a Web server.

Web Page A single file as viewed within a Web browser. Several Web pages linked together represent a website.